Tompkins County

Tompkins County

New York

Images of Work and Play

Municipal Historians of Tompkins County
and the Tompkins County Historian

The History Press

Published by The History Press
Charleston, SC 29403
www.historypress.net

First published 2009

Manufactured in the United States

ISBN 978.1.59629.684.8

Library of Congress Cataloging-in-Publication Data

Tompkins County, New York : images of work and play / Municipal Historians of Tompkins County and the Tompkins County Historian.
p. cm.
Includes bibliographical references and index.
"Carol Kammen, Tompkins County Historian"--Pref.
ISBN 978-1-59629-684-8 (alk. paper)
1. Tompkins County (N.Y.)--History. 2. Tompkins County (N.Y.)--Pictorial works. I. Kammen, Carol, 1937-
F127.T7T66 2009
974.7'7104--dc22
2009029195

To those who came before us who made collections, researched, preserved and wrote our local history.

CONTENTS

PREFACE

Open the pages of *Tompkins County, New York: Images of Work and Play* and discover our local past—people you might remember; names you may have heard and people engaged in activities you might have enjoyed. The appointed historians of Tompkins County, their deputies and an ever-expanding number of people collaborated to create this book of images showing what life here was once like and how we have evolved from that other time into our own while retaining important distinctive qualities.

New York State is unique in its requirement that each incorporated community with a population greater than four hundred appoint a municipal historian. The original idea in 1919 was that these historians would gather information about the veterans of the Great War, then returning home from Europe, and also document the passing of veterans of the Civil War, rapidly declining in number. Over time the job description for these historians expanded. Municipal historians took on the care of local documents, searched for materials in need of preservation and found various ways to promote community knowledge. Appointed historians interpret their jobs in ways that suit their interests and skills.

Municipal officers—usually town supervisors, village and city mayors and county administrators—have the power of appointment, but they also bring their own opinions about the duties of the local historian. Some municipal historians receive compensation and office space while others do not. Some engage in the preservation of cemeteries; conduct genealogical research; organize and preserve local records; or write newspaper articles, pamphlets and books. Some speak at community celebrations, picnics, on television or at town board meetings. There are currently over 1,300 appointed historians across New York State.

Since 2000, the appointed historian from each municipality within Tompkins County and an assistant or deputy have met as the Municipal Historians of Tompkins County (MHTC). We expanded our circle by inviting others who care about our local past to contribute to our ongoing conversation about local history. There are short biographies of everyone who worked on this project at the end of this book.

At our meetings we discuss new research materials, interesting historical topics and methods of teasing information from locally available sources. We share what we learn and talk about historical topics within a framework of the knowledge and experience of other places in the county. For example, the history of abolition touched all parts of the county, some people responding with enthusiasm and others with concern and caution; seeing this historical topic within the framework of the entire county is very important. So, too, the Depression of the 1930s touched everyone in the county and needs to be looked at in its larger context. Not everyone lost a job but many did. Some lost their homes, but others thought themselves little touched by the economic crisis. It is good to understand such events with the aid of others.

The MHTC also aims to increase county residents' enjoyment and understanding of this place—how communities came into existence, the names on the landscape—and to explain the area to the many visitors who come here. In 2002, we created a brochure of historical organizations and sites located within the county. In 2004, we published *Place Names in Tompkins County* with support from the Community Foundation of Tompkins County and the Tompkins County Foundation. That book is available at The History Center and in local bookstores and has been downloaded onto the Tompkins County Historian's website, where it is available electronically at www.tompkins-co.org/historian/placenames/index.html. In addition, in 2007 we created "Touring the Towns of Tompkins County" brochures devoted to historical, geological and special features to be found in the towns of Tompkins County. The Strategic Tourism Planning Board of Tompkins County supported this project, and these brochures, too, have been placed on the County Historian's Internet site. We have found working together productive and joyful.

This book came about when an editor from The History Press asked me to create a book of images of the county. This seemed like a perfect project for the Municipal Historians. At a meeting we discussed and then voted to embark on the book. We determined that our focus would be on people of the county and that the pictures would range from the 1890s to 1960. We also decided that we wanted to show how people of the county have lived their lives here.

A month after that meeting, we faced piles of pictures from historical societies and municipal archives, many from The History Center and some from private collections brought in for consideration. While most people warn that too many cooks in the kitchen at one time spoil the outcome, we had more than twenty people swirling about a room sorting images, discovering and advocating one image or another, and delighting in seeing pictures well known to them or others never before seen.

We divided the pictures by category and sorted for balance and interest and geographical distribution. Unlike similar books, these images are not grouped by town but are organized by topic, so that the pictures of any one place or from a particular collection are scattered throughout. We have included the location of the original photograph in the credit line beneath each picture.

We all were involved in creating captions to explain the images. Some of the photographs we used had information attached, but many did not—just as many of the pictures in family photograph albums do not have names written in. Donna Eschenbrenner, archivist at The History Center, led a determined group of volunteers to research the information that accompanies pictures from that rich archive.

While the captions were being researched and written, Rosemarie Tucker began the process of scanning the old photographs. At the June meeting of the MHTC, we engaged in checking our lists and checking them twice to ensure that pictures and captions matched and that the captions were as complete as possible. Mindful of the reader's need for clarity and careful to preserve the information and tone of captions and essays, our team of editors set to work.

Finally, by late June, we sent the press a compact disc with the pictures, a file containing all of the captions and another with the text. The first phase of putting together this book was done.

Work and Play Themes

In creating *Tompkins County, New York: Images of Work and Play*, we wanted to bring attention to photographs that focused on people rather than on our institutional or even on our architectural heritage—these topics can be found in other books. We included pictures of people who lived here: in the houses we now occupy and on the farms that ring the county, as well as the people who worked in gardens established long ago. We aimed at continuities to be found in the county: those things that endure and that continue to concern us. Work has always been essential, but there has always been play, and the topics link people today to those who lived here before.

In addition to the continuities of life, we wanted readers to see how things have changed over time—how horses and carriages gave way to rickety-looking horseless carriages and how the automobile became modern. We thought it important to focus on occupations, such as blacksmithing or working in small factories that once were common throughout the county but are no longer found here. We wondered if we could suggest how we have become the people we are today.

The photographs come from a variety of archives, and some from private collections. We know that there are many photographs still in private hands—of uncles who came to visit, of children in the yard, of a new automobile or holiday event—and that many of these can be found in attics, bottom drawers, photograph albums and, sadly, in garages. Many of these pictures, taken to capture a moment, were only of importance to families and friends. Yet, as the years have gone by, those snapshots have become historical documents that capture a particular time and place. They add to what we know about the county's past, and they lead us to understand people who have lived here before. They help us see change created by individual will, by technology, or by fad or historical force. Many of our historical organizations would welcome the opportunity to copy and add pictures from family scrapbooks to their collections. Images are our aides de memoirs, our nudges about things that matter—or once mattered, though they might no longer mean the same things. Photographs remind us of our connection to time and place, of continuity and change. These photographs connect us to one another.

This book has been a joy to create. There is a genuine pleasure in working with people who care about one another and whose goal is to create something of value for the community. There is a happiness to be found in having colleagues for whom the answer to most issues is shared laughter and then a willingness to dig in to help.

We hope you enjoy this book.

Carol Kammen
Tompkins County Historian

INTRODUCTION

The first thing that most people say when they arrive in Tompkins County and look at our beautiful hills and valleys is "It's so green here!" Part of this is due to our enviable position on the planet, in the heart of the Finger Lakes. Part of it is because of our deep agricultural roots; farmland still makes up a large part of the county, and even those who don't make a living off the land appreciate the rural atmosphere and lifestyle. At a party the other night, a young lady returning from law school in Boston was telling me how happy she was to be back. "The city has its attractions and purposes," she explained, "but it's not home."

People have been making their homes in this area for thousands of years. The Iroquois hunted, fished, planted gardens and raised families, with allowances for changing technology, much as we do today. While they had somewhat different concerns and expectations, the Iroquois, too, wanted their children to do well, and they enjoyed time spent with friends and in community activities. Theirs was an oral tradition, and much of what we know about them comes from artifacts, stories handed down from generation to generation. Most of the stories, when committed to writing, were filtered through the understanding of Europeans, who transcribed the accounts and whose descendents now walk these hills. By the time photography, with its ability to show truths, was invented, few of these First Peoples were still living in Tompkins County.

Photographs, especially before the digital age, can be more honest and unbiased than written or spoken information. Still, they were taken and subsequently preserved for a reason. By luck or design, we have these photographic records of the past because someone had the means and motivation to save them. Whether documenting an event or showing off a new family member, they often have something to tell us about the time and the reason the image was taken, and we can contrast that with the time that has passed since the camera shutter opened and closed. Yet, one must admit that what, exactly, photographs have to tell us is often still something of a mystery.

Each of the photos in this book is a story—sometimes clear, sometimes more vague—with its own who, what, when, where and why. It's easy to see why some of these pictures were taken and impossible to know the reason behind others. For some pictures the "who" has been lost to the ages. It's fascinating to ponder the meaning that is to be found in each photo.

This book started with historians from the towns in Tompkins County getting together with piles of photos from their town archives. Other pictures came to us through private donations. Some had been printed in a newspaper, and some were taken by professional photographers, but most were taken by amateurs. Did the photograph illustrate one of our subject headings for the chapters? Was it clear and detailed enough to reproduce well for the book? Did it duplicate the subject matter of other photos that would be in the book? Was it an image already well known in the county?

There were enough pictures for several books, and it was tough to sort them out and make final decisions. But that was the pleasure of working on this book. There were photos from the Town of Caroline that I had seen long ago but had forgotten. There were photos dug out of scrapbooks that hadn't been opened in decades that were new to me and will be new to almost everyone who opens this book. I was fascinated and, to be frank, occasionally envious of the photos from other towns. Speaking as a photographer, there were several I wish I had taken myself. Some were striking in their artistic merit; some had important news to convey. Every one of them was a glimpse into the lives of people who lived in the same places we do now—people who, just as with the Iroquois so long ago, raised families, planted gardens, walked these green hills and gazed in wonder at the night sky. What readers will find in the pages of this book is a visual delight.

In our family albums or in boxes stowed away in our attics, we all have pictures of babies and deep snowfalls, weddings and new cars. We communicate across the miles and years with photographs, mailing (or nowadays e-mailing) pictures back and forth. The photos in this book show wedding suppers, workmen, kids having fun and a grandson and grandfather at the grandmother's grave. Not all of the people can be identified, and sometimes we only know a small part of their stories. Thanks to these pictures, though, and thanks to whoever took the time to save them, they are ours to wonder about and enjoy.

These pictures tell the stories of people much like ourselves. While the clothes have changed and horse-drawn wagons have given way to cars, the patterns of their lives and the things that they cared about remain familiar. Some of the stories told in the photographs are dramatic: tales of floods, fires, train wrecks and car accidents. Other pictures document everyday occurrences: men and women at work, family picnics, religious observances, children at school and people playing with their pets. In these common moments, it is easy to see our lives and even to put ourselves in the picture. Of course, some of the jobs depicted don't exist any more: cutting ice and storing it away for summer cooling has given way to refrigeration technology (we hardly say "ice box" anymore). Yet other jobs—such as that of the draftsmen, manure spreaders, sauerkraut factory workers and lumberjacks—have merely changed techniques.

For all of the changes between then and now, these photographs do communicate to us. They tell us something about how people lived then. They tell us a lot about how we live today.

While the photographic process was invented in 1826 by Joseph Nicéphore Niépce, a French lithographer, it wasn't until 1839 that Louis-Jacques-Mandé Daguerre, a French painter, astonished the world with his new invention, a more practical way of taking pictures. Still, registering images by the use of light was not easy. Working with a fifty-pound camera, silver-plated sheets of copper and iodine vapor, Daguerre recorded images. He developed them using toxic mercury vapor to fix the image and equally toxic chemicals to remove the unexposed silver to reveal the picture. The technology then did not allow for moving subjects as exposure times were long. The next fifty years showed steady progress in photographic technology. Because creating what came to be called daguerreotypes required heavy gear, chemicals and fragile glass plates, the task was mainly in the hands of professionals or very dedicated amateurs. A studio portrait was a planned event, at first available only to those of independent means. The portrait was meant to mark an important occasion, such as a marriage or a birth, and was a means of demonstrating hard-won prosperity. Even the Civil War photographs of Matthew Brady were posed; exposure times and preparation needed to make a print required careful thought.

Family albums, the source of some pictures in this book, benefited from George Eastman's 1889 invention of a box camera with flexible film. One would purchase a camera already loaded with one hundred frames of roll film. After all the pictures were taken, the camera containing the film was shipped to the factory in Rochester, New York, and the film was developed by Eastman's employees. Prints were made and mailed back to the photographer, who may have already purchased another camera loaded with one hundred frames to begin the cycle anew. Photography became more spontaneous, and it was no longer the province of professionals.

Families continued to pose for studio photos, and of course they still do. Yet people were also able to express themselves and communicate via photographs in ways that had never been open to them before. By taking photography out of the studio and putting it in the hands of ordinary people, the kind of pictures produced changed. We were finally able to see how people really lived.

Birthday parties, picnics, the beginnings and endings of trips, even Mom feeding the chickens—all of these events were faithfully recorded. Often people are shown wearing their everyday clothing, but sometimes they are in costume. Photos of amateur theatricals appear, and adults as well as children are displayed in makeshift finery. Band members are arrayed in uniforms heavy with braid, pant legs creased and instruments shining in the sun. Children are seen playing in the garden, enjoying sleigh rides or driving their pony cart. Pets get involved, and we see them sleeping on the porch, pulling a wagon or dressed up for a parade. Prized flowers are documented. Outside the tight control of a studio, life happens. Many of my favorite pictures are these spontaneous slices of life.

Some things, even in the oldest of these photos, seem obvious. Others depend on a knowledge of the subject. A farmer looking at one of these pictures will observe the time of year and equipment and will know which crops are being harvested. An office worker will call the animal in the picture a cow, but the farmer will see a steer almost ready for market. The psychologist may not know that they're standing in front of a hay rake but might notice that the humans are comfortably holding hands with one another.

Some of the photos show activities, such as women driving automobiles, a surprising activity in another time. A senior citizen, however, might recall that when her mother learned to drive, she was the only female in town trusted with something so mechanical. One of the most poignant pictures in this book is that of the descendents of an African American slave and white master, sitting together companionably on the front porch. It is a slice of reality that is difficult to contemplate, and the emotional effect is likely shared by us all.

With digital cameras and telephones that create videos, photographs have become ubiquitous. With computer programs to edit digital images, hair color, waistlines, backgrounds and even facial expressions can be changed. Photos now often also stay in cameras or on computers, unprinted and unavailable to those without direct access. While I appreciate the artistic possibilities and the ability from my home in Tompkins County to see images of my granddaughter moments after her birth in Wisconsin, I wonder if future generations will be deprived of the fun we have had while handling old photos, daydreaming about times past and deciding which images to share.

While they might not all rise to the grandeur of Ansel Adams's "Moonrise, Hernandez, New Mexico," the pictures in this book and the lives that they depict are no less important. Like the photos you take, they present the stories of those who have worked, played and lived in Tompkins County. They are our history. I hope you enjoy them as much as we did. For most people, when asked what material possession they would grab if there were a fire at their home, the reply is usually "my photos." What they really mean is "my history" or "my stories." Enjoy your stories. Keep them safe. Your family and, yes, future historians will thank you.

Patricia Brhel

AT WORK

While we often think of our Tompkins County ancestors as farmers, agriculture is only part of their shared story. From the earliest days in the nineteenth century, many professional men, such as doctors, lawyers and preachers, were residents of the county. Factory or mill owners and workers were also found wherever there was ample water power. Each village had its own storekeeper, blacksmith, stable owner, sawyer, schoolteacher and iceman; taken together, their labors kept the community running smoothly. In towns and villages of the late nineteenth and early twentieth century, there were people employed in jobs that do not exist anymore, such as glove makers and cigar rollers, or in jobs that now only exist in certain parts of the country, such as Amish buggy makers and farriers. Other employments, such as delivering the mail, have changed their modes of transportation from the horse and buggy to the horseless carriage but are otherwise the same as they were fifty or one hundred years ago.

The labor of mothering and the toil of domestic life were as much facts of life in villages as in the countryside. Moreover, even in the early years of the county, some women became teachers, boardinghouse proprietors, washerwomen, milliners, seamstresses or bakers. Even children in town had regular chores, such as sweeping out the family store, feeding the chickens in the backyard or hauling in stove wood.

A peek at old photographs reveals many of the ways that men, women and children have contributed to the life of their communities by laboring in the shops, factories, homes and streets of our towns and villages.

Mr. Adam is pictured in Joseph C. Burritt's garden on North Albany Street in Ithaca. Burritt, who lived from 1817 to 1889, operated his family's jewelry shop on Ithaca's State Street for fifty years. In the 1860s, he photographed Ithacans, their homes and area gorges and waterfalls, using the early collodion "wet plate" process. His artful photographs are among the earliest taken in Ithaca. Nothing more is known about Mr. Adam. *Courtesy The History Center in Tompkins County, GPF N6.26A.*

Frank Howland began blacksmithing in 1910 and continued in his trade for seventeen years. His first shop was located near the South Lansing Fire Station. In 1927, he moved into the building that became the Red and White grocery. Frank was the proprietor of the store for many years. *Courtesy Lansing Historical Association.*

In 1904, a Pennsylvania crew of woodcutters, with cook and a child, arrived at Locke's holdings to cut a large woodlot in Pine Woods. They stayed in the woods in an old cabin. Pine Woods is the area west of New York State Route 13 after New York State Route 366 joins from Etna and goes on to Varna. The forest, on the south side of the highway, is located between Baker Hill and Mineah Roads and extends up to Mount Pleasant. *Gift of Gladys Locke, Dryden Town Historical Society Archives.*

Starting in 1905, Slaterville Road from Ithaca to Richford was widened and macadam sealant laid down. In 1908, the improvement had reached as far as West Slaterville, and when work started in the spring of 1909, when this photograph was taken, the stone crusher was located in a field just west of the hamlet of Slaterville on the south side of the road. Stone from the fields on both sides of the road was crushed and used in the making of the macadam. This structure no longer stands. *Courtesy Higgins Album, Town of Caroline Historical Room.*

Three men outside the West Danby Lehigh Valley Railroad Station, located at the foot of Station Road, probably in the early 1900s. The station no longer exists but was located on a level area on the northeast side of the current track crossing. The current home of the Mel Westmiller family was at one time the ticket and wait station for the Lehigh Valley Railroad. *Courtesy Wayne Myers from the William Ellis Collection.*

Around the turn of the twentieth century, men cut ice from local farm ponds and also from Cayuga Lake to be stored in icehouses, where it was packed in sawdust for summer use. Francis Allen worked taking ice off the lake during the year the lake froze all the way across and the men could drive horses and bobsleds from one side to the other. *Courtesy Lansing Historical Association.*

A bridge constructed by men, a steam engine and horsepower crossed Taughannock Creek, west of New York State Route 89, 1926. The Jones property on Cayuga Lake was purchased by New York State in 1925 and became part of the sixty-four-acre Taughannock Falls State Park, providing access to the lake in the Town of Ulysses. *Courtesy Ulysses Historical Society, PA1922.*

Henley Hunter's log yard was located behind the old Bailey Home at 71 West Main Street, Dryden. Dewitt Hiles and Mr. Duell are shown using a device called a peel in May 1905. Bark slabs sold to the Kennedy Brothers Tannery on Lake Street and Tannery Creek were used to cure hides in the preparation of leather. *Courtesy the Nettie Hunt Collection, Dryden Town Historical Society Archives.*

This circa 1900 photograph shows a worker at the National Salt Company in Myers in the town of Lansing wheeling a load of salt to be dumped on the large pile in the room below. By 1904, the plant consisted of fifteen boilers, two pans, six grainers, four wells and other necessary buildings and equipment. The influx of workers, many from Syria who came with their families, necessitated the enlargement of the Ludlowville Union School. *Courtesy Lansing Historical Association.*

This image of workers posing in front of a paper mill on Fall Creek in Ithaca was taken before 1900. Papermaking began at this location in 1818. Mack and Andrus operated the upper and lower mills until 1887. After a series of owners, the Read Paper Company bought the lower mill in 1926. Ample water power in Tompkins County attracted industry. *Courtesy The History Center in Tompkins County, GPF J30.40.*

When the Caroline Methodist-Episcopal Church was built in 1895, the Ladies' Aid Society wanted to put in a lawn. Mr. Silsbee said he would "fit" the ground if the society would plant and harvest potatoes on the land the first year. The members agreed, and he plowed and dragged the ground. The women planted, weeded, hilled and dug the potatoes, after which Mr. Silsbee seeded it down to grass. *Courtesy People in Caroline Album, Town of Caroline Historical Room.*

Shown here is a railroad train in West Danby in 1909. The caption reads that the engine crews posed for a picture while working at the Thatcher Cut, a line relocation project on the old Geneva, Ithaca and Sayre Railroad southeast of West Danby. The project was finished in September 1909. *Courtesy the William F. Ellis Collection, Danby.*

The Cornell Incubator Manufacturing Company was an outgrowth of the chicken farming ventures of Ithacans Edward Wyckoff and Ezra Cornell, grandson of the founder of Cornell University. Incorporated in 1900, the company was located in the same Brindley Street factory in Ithaca that later housed the Thomas-Morse Aircraft Corporation. Farmers used incubators when there were not enough broody hens to hatch eggs. *Courtesy The History Center in Tompkins County, GPF J30.111.*

Workers at the Reed & Montgomery Bindery of Ithaca are pictured here about 1900. Owned by F.G. Reed and W.W. Montgomery, the bindery was located at 118–124 South Tioga Street. "All kinds of Blank Books ruled and bound to pattern at Reed & Montgomery's," read one of their advertisements in the *Ithaca City Directory* of 1899. By the turn of the twentieth century, women could often be found in small manufacturing enterprises. *Courtesy The History Center in Tompkins County, GPF J30.15.*

In 1914, brothers William T. and Oliver Thomas moved their airplane factory, the Thomas-Morse Aircraft Corporation, from Bath, New York, to Brindley Street in Ithaca near the Cayuga Lake inlet. At the Thomas Brothers Aeroplane Company and Aviation School, they produced innovative biplanes for the U.S. Army Signal Corps and the British Admiralty. Here workers posed next to planes in the earliest stages of production. *Courtesy The History Center in Tompkins County, GPF J30.144.*

In 1917, the Thomas Brothers Aeroplane Company and Ithaca's Morse Chain merged to form the Thomas-Morse Aircraft Corporation. One of its greatest planes was the S-4-C "Tommy" Scout, a fast, maneuverable advanced trainer. More than six hundred were made during World War I, and afterward many were sold to flying schools. The assembly crew for the Scout was a large, highly skilled group, and they pose here in 1917 with one of their planes. *Courtesy The History Center in Tompkins County, GPF J45.33.*

Workers are shown testing engines on the S-4-C Scout at Ithaca's Thomas-Morse Aircraft factory. The engine was an eighty-horsepower Le Rhone, a rotary engine in which the crankshaft remained stationary and all of the cylinders revolved around it. In 1929, the Thomas-Morse Aircraft Corporation was sold to Consolidated Aircraft and moved to Buffalo, and a significant chapter in Ithaca aviation history was closed. *Courtesy The History Center in Tompkins County, GPF J45.28.*

Biggs Memorial Hospital was a tuberculosis facility located on the west shore of Cayuga Lake, near the present location of the Cayuga Medical Center. "H" Building was the Pediatric Ward. Pictured with their charges on the sun porch are three nurses, including, on the right, B. Smith, J. Halltower and Rose Vicarelli Frost. The children were allowed to wear their street clothes to lessen the reminder of their ailments. *Courtesy Roger and Joan Frost Grant.*

This stone mill was built on West Main Street, Dryden, near Highland Avenue in 1836. In the 1910s, the name changed from the Dryden Blanket Company to the Atlantic Woolen Mill, and the workers made "shoddy" out of reprocessed wool. During World War I, shoddy was woven into khaki-colored blankets for doughboys. War's end caused the company's collapse. Four women are shown with their scissors; one is holding a very large pair of shears and was probably the group leader. *Front, from left*: Irene Lord Pugsley and Ada Jennison Brown. *Middle, from left*: _____ Bailey Swarts, Cornelia Warren Pugsley and Catherine DeVinney. *Back, from left*: Jennie Wheeler and Eva Rolfe Green. *Courtesy the Nettie Hunt Collection, Dryden Town Historical Society Archives.*

This July 1913 photo shows a group of men who worked for Otto Petermann. They are surveying for a development in the Village of Groton now known as Pasadena Avenue. Born in Switzerland in 1876, Petermann, from 1909 to 1926, was the chief designer for Corona Typewriter Company when he established his own consulting, design and manufacturing business in Groton. *Courtesy Rosemarie Palmer Tucker.*

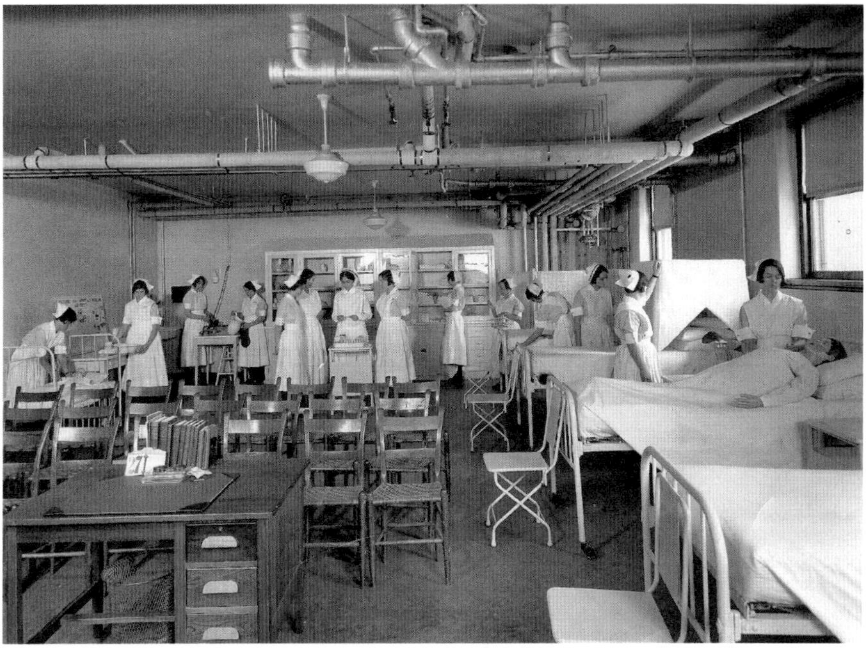

Nurses and possibly nursing students are shown here in this undated image of the Ithaca City Hospital on Quarry Street. The hospital was built in 1912 and served to train nurses. The hospital served Ithaca and the surrounding area until it closed in 1958. Nursing, like teaching, was one of the professions open to women in the early years of the twentieth century. Lecture rooms for nursing students were provided in the construction plans for the Ithaca City Hospital. *Courtesy The History Center in Tompkins County, GPF T10.41.*

This photograph of Charles Dorsey and his mule on Main Street, Trumansburg, was taken sometime in the 1920s. The Dorsey family settled in Trumansburg in the 1840s, one of the first African American families to make their home in the village. They lived on Lake Street, known locally as Dorsey Hill. *Courtesy Ulysses Historical Society, PI1261.*

This thrashing machine was manufactured by the Groton Bridge & Manufacturing Company. It is shown being hoisted for loading on the train to be delivered to its destination. Established in 1847 from a single blacksmith shop and a few frame buildings, the Groton Bridge Company made bridges, thrashing machines, road crushers and other products. *Courtesy The History Center in Tompkins County.*

Godley's store, located on the south side of Main Street in Newfield, offered residents a wide selection of tinware, stoves and general hardware, among other things. Dustpans, pots and locks are prominently displayed in the windows. This 1909 photograph shows Monte Godley in the doorway, his brother Leon and their father, Samuel N. Godley, standing proudly in front of their establishment. *Courtesy Mary Smith, Newfield.*

The Monarch Road Roller Company of Groton manufactured this machine. In 1913, the company had a government order for six machines, shipping four to the Philippines and two to paving contractors in Brazil. The company manufactured steamrollers, threshers, traction engines and other heavy road machinery that were shipped from Groton by rail. The company closed in November 1917. The man in the lower left with a mustache is Otto Petermann. *Courtesy Rosemarie Palmer Tucker.*

When the Rothschild brothers—Jacob, Daniel and Isaac—founded a department store in Ithaca in 1882, they did not know it would become one of the city's most loved institutions. Known for its quality merchandise, Rothschild's remained at the center of downtown life until its closing in 1982. This interesting photo, teeming with men, equipment and supplies, was taken during an early remodeling of the store in 1913–15. *Courtesy The History Center in Tompkins County, GPF J10.43.*

At the extreme southwest corner of the Town of Dryden is an area known as Bethel Grove. Running between Slaterville Road (now New York State Route 79) and the Coddington Road is German Cross Road. Yonkin's Store was a small white building with a large Tydol Gas sign in front. Operated by Steward and Caroline Yonkin Wilson, this view shows Caroline behind the counter in 1925. She later married Harold Rightmyer, and he also helped run the store and the station until the early 1950s. Note the supply of Kellogg's Corn Flakes! *Courtesy the Roger Yonkin Collection, Dryden Town Historical Society Archives.*

Workers stripped loose leaves from cabbages at Lang's Sauerkraut Factory before cutting and processing them. Rose Bell Harvey Wallenbeck is seated at the far right. This photograph was taken about 1920. The factory opened in 1912 and closed about 1954. It was located off King Street, west of the Lehigh Valley Railroad Station, Trumansburg, in the Town of Ulysses. *Courtesy Ulysses Historical Society, IND 217.*

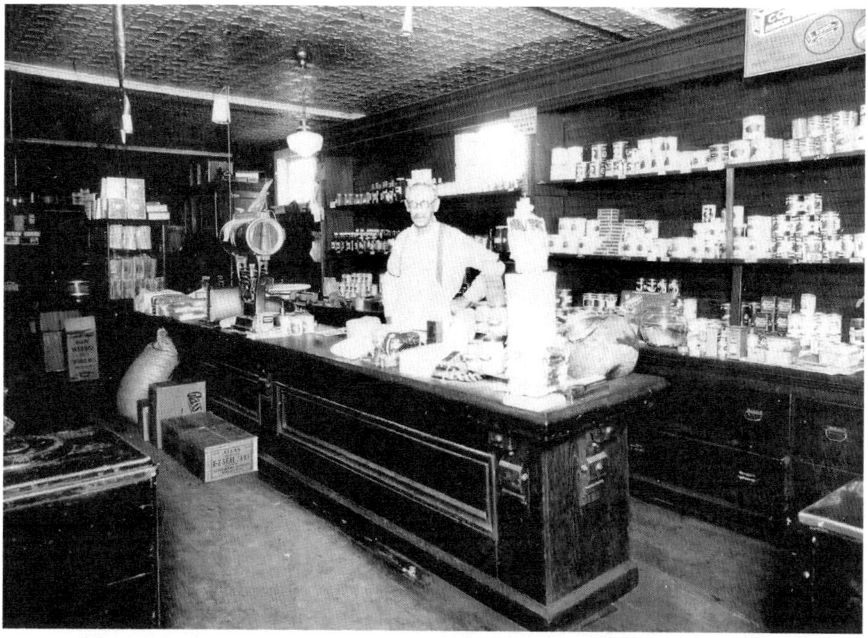

In this late 1930s photo, Art Tubbs stands behind the counter of his Danby store at 1850 Danby Road. Observe the ornate pressed-tin ceiling in the Tubbs Store, the scale for weighing bulk goods and the brown paper roll for wrapping purchases. Canning jars are at the ready in front of the sales counter. *Courtesy Susie Benjamin.*

John Williamson, the community barber, in his barbershop at 15 Railroad Street in the Village of Freeville about 1920. Note the photographer's reflection in the mirror behind him. *Courtesy Joan Manning.*

The Peters-Morse Manufacturing Company was founded in 1919 to produce adding machines. The company used the Allen-Wales Corporation to market and sell its machines; the two eventually merged after the 1929 stock market crash and became very successful. In 1943, the company was sold to National Cash Register's adding machine division and is located on South Hill in Ithaca. *Courtesy The History Center in Tompkins County, GPF J30.175.*

Above: Shown here are the employees of Petermann's Design and Manufacturing Company. Formed in 1926, Otto Petermann was an inventor and developer. From 1909 to 1926, he was the chief designer for the Corona Typewriter Company and held the patent for the Corona 3 Folding Typewriter. *Courtesy Rosemarie Palmer Tucker.*

Left: Beloved Newfield schoolteacher Margaret Van Riper on the ladder with her parents, Fred Van Riper and Hattie Smith Payne Van Riper, in their summer garden, showing off their gardening skills with these huge sunflowers. Margaret Van Riper taught three generations of Newfield students in her forty-year career lasting from 1924 to 1965. She is remembered fondly by students as being "stern with heart." *Courtesy the Collection Archives Alive, Newfield Public Library and Newfield Historical Society.*

The Danby road crew about 1931, from left, includes an individual believed to be Jabe Brown; Rick Nelson, in front of the shovel-boss; Frank Chaffee, in shovel; unidentified man leaning on shovel; Herb Bennett on the back of the shovel; Hershal Henderson seated to the left in the truck; John Elliott seated to the right in the truck; and a man believed to be Jon Sorance standing outside of the truck. *Courtesy Mary Elliott Howard.*

Born in South Carolina, James L. Gibbs first came to Ithaca in 1935 to become the first director of the newly built Southside Community Center. Trained as a social worker, Gibbs, a tireless advocate for Ithaca's African American community in an age when opportunities for blacks were severely limited, is pictured here in his office at Southside in 1939 speaking with Frank White, as Carolyn Dean types in the foreground. *Courtesy The History Center in Tompkins County, FBO-0015.87.*

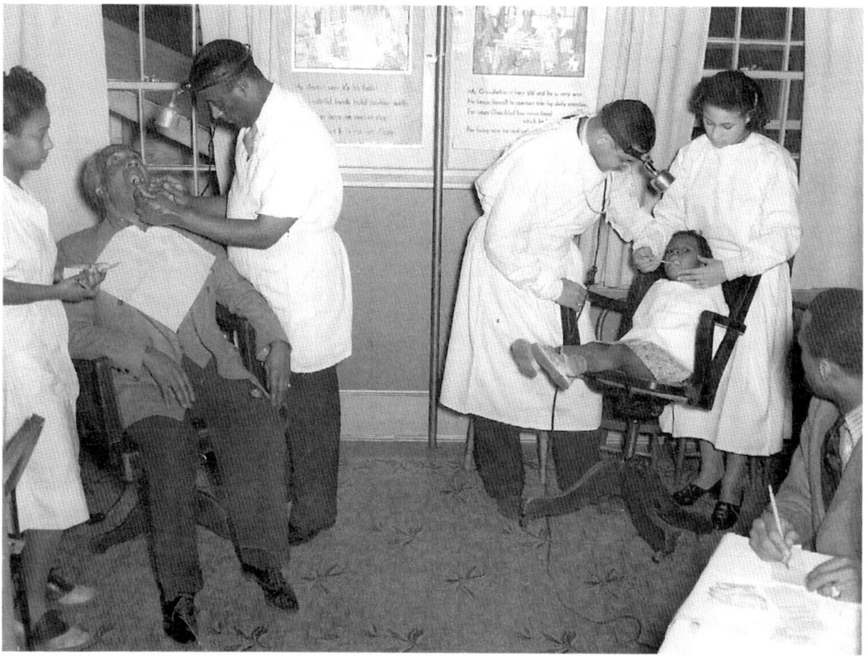

Above: In the 1930s, government-sponsored National Negro Health Week initiatives were meant to encourage good health practices in the African American community. Ithaca was among many American cities to participate. James Gibbs, director of the Southside Community Center, brought medical professionals to the area for their expertise and the living example they would set for African American children. Dr. G. Alex Galvin and Dr. Albert Johnson are pictured in 1939, as they examine local patients. *Courtesy The History Center in Tompkins County, FBO-0015.29.*

Right: By 1943, the demands of World War II caused an acute nursing shortage. To answer the need, the federal government established the Cadet Nurse Corps within the Public Health Service. Doris Place (1922–1966), shown here, was a resident of Enfield who became a cadet nurse. She earned a degree in biological sciences from Cornell University and her bachelor of science in nursing at the New York Cornell Medical Center. She earned her master's degree at Columbia Teachers College in 1955, and she retired as an administrator for Medical Sciences and registered nurse at the University of Arkansas. *Courtesy Town of Enfield historian.*

Ithaca Gun Company workers were major contributors to the war effort during the 1940s, making approximately half of the U.S. Army's .45-caliber pistols. A preponderance of female workers in factory jobs was common during World War II, when men were off serving in the armed forces. Note the sign in the background of this image cautioning workers to stay focused on their tasks at hand. *Courtesy The History Center in Tompkins County, GPF J40.5.*

During a peak in the 1920s, the Ithaca Gun Company produced fifty-two thousand weapons per year, including double-barreled shotguns renowned for their workmanship for hunters. Ithaca Gun was founded in 1883 along the rim of Fall Creek gorge. Falling demand finally ended the company's century as one of Ithaca's leading industries. Today, Ithaca Guns are collectors' items. *Courtesy The History Center in Tompkins County, GPF J40.3.*

Above: Duke Mulks was a Luce Dairy deliveryman, shown with his new Vivco, a stand-up drive truck. William A. Luce, the owner's young son, is shown standing in the truck in Jacksonville in 1949. His grandfather, William A. Luce, founded this Ithaca company in 1917. The first deliveries to the Town of Ulysses, Village of Trumansburg and Jacksonville hamlet occurred in 1952. Crowley Foods bought out the dairy in 1970. *Courtesy Virginia V. Luce Collection.*

Right: Kenneth Rice and Leon Courtemanche are pictured in the Leigh Valley Railroad Station in Freeville in 1958. Built along the Southern Central Railroad line about 1870, the Freeville station served as an important hub for both commuter and freight transit throughout the neighboring areas of Cortland, Ithaca and Auburn. Rice, seen in the background, served as the station's telegrapher beginning in 1937. *Courtesy The History Center in Tompkins County, GPF T15.30.*

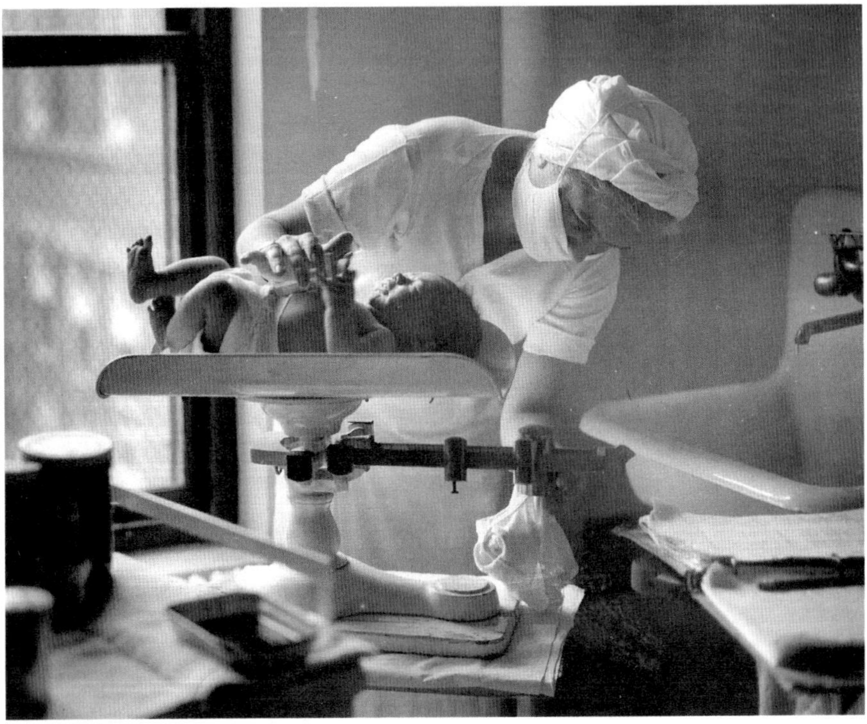

The Ithaca City Hospital on South Quarry Street was the main facility in the area. In 1958, medical care moved to its present site on Trumansburg Road. This picture shows a nurse weighing a newborn in the pediatric ward sometime in the 1950s. The juxtaposition of the carefully masked nurse in her neat white uniform and the wiggling infant, legs kicking and hands reaching, makes for an engaging and endearing image. *Courtesy The History Center in Tompkins County, 80.130.977.*

This picture, taken by C. Hadley Smith of Ithaca, a local photographer, shows the men and machinery used in the rock salt mine far below Cayuga Lake. The first mine, begun in 1914, did not find a good grade of salt, but in 1921 the Cayuga Rock Salt Company founded by Frank I. Bolton and John W. Shannon worked a new level of good salt, and the mine has been in operation ever since. The Cargill Company bought the salt company in 1970, modernizing the facility and boring an additional shaft from the bottom 2,300-foot level to the surface. *Courtesy Lansing Historical Association.*

Above: Catherine Hilker (left) was born in Germany in 1875 and homesteaded in the Dakota Territory until 1925, when her family relocated to Tompkins County. She is dressed here for berry picking with her daughter-in-law, Edna Stamp Hilker; this picture was taken in front of Catherine's home on Coddington Road in the town of Caroline. *Courtesy Terry Hilker Donlick.*

Left: Martha Dickson, bookkeeper, and Jim Crimmins, owner of the Trumansburg Foodliner grocery store, which was located on Main Street, are shown. Crimmins often came up with novel marketing ideas. Here he is seen about 1959 with an instant water display. *Courtesy Ulysses Historical Society, BI.597.*

A worker stitches a leather bag at R. Appel, Inc. in the 1950s, watched by company superintendent Oscar T. Swenson at right. Known by Ithacans as "the pocket book factory," the company opened in 1934. At one time it made close to 1,800 handbags per day, sold throughout the United States and Canada, including its "Plasticflex" bag. Imports and imitation leather took their toll on R. Appel's sales, and the factory closed its doors about 1959. *Courtesy The History Center in Tompkins County, GPF J31.5.*

After the opening of Cornell University in 1868, the population in Tompkins County expanded. The establishment of the Ithaca street railway system in the 1880s provided convenient transportation about the city. By the 1920s, there was extensive house building on East Hill, in Cornell Heights and Cayuga Heights and then in the Town of Ithaca. Here a construction crew pauses in their work for this undated image. *Courtesy The History Center in Tompkins County, GPF I10.42.*

ON THE FARM

Through the years, agriculture has undergone change with seemingly little public notice. Yet, those employed in the care of land and livestock have always appreciated and been well aware of advances in technology, which made labor easier and farms more productive. These resulted in changes for farm families as well.

In the twentieth century, long hours of labor in fields and barns were significantly reduced. This also affected the number of agricultural laborers employed in the United States, which dropped from nearly 40 percent to about 3 percent by the end of the century. Local farmers first used horsepower to till fields, which these photographs show, but horses were quickly replaced by mechanized machines that accomplished farm tasks with greater efficiency. Gasoline tractors with rubber tires replaced early steel-wheeled tractors. With improvements in tilling equipment, fertilizers, seed and a greater understanding of horticultural practices, less labor is now required to produce larger yields. These changes granted farmers and their families more leisure time. The Grange League Federation, which flourished for a time in Tompkins County, offered agricultural education and social occasions.

Ralph Waldo Emerson wrote in "Farming" that the "first farmer was the first man, and all historic nobility rests on possession and use of the land." For Emerson the agricultural life contained "in all ways its ancient charm." In the pictures collected here, the faces of those who tilled the land glisten with obvious pride of accomplishment.

This group gathered grain at the Truman Baker farm in 1869 near Ridgecrest Road in the Town of Danby. *From left*: an unidentified woman, the family dog, Oscar Baker and L.B.R. and LeVerne Baker. The hand scythe pictured at the right has a sharp blade on the bottom with three rake tines on the top to cut and gather at the same time. The grain was raked into piles with a rake similar to the one pictured to the left, tied around the middle and left in the field to dry. *Courtesy Jack Baker and Bob Snyder.*

Marcus DeLafayette Shaver, also known as "Coon," is seen plowing the garden at his home at 4 Mill Street in the Village of Freeville, about 1900. The large elm tree in the distance was on property owned by John Sager. *Courtesy Joan Manning.*

Around the turn of the twentieth century, people brought raw milk to the Slaterville Creamery by both horse and oxen teams. Spoke and wheel factories provided maintenance for carriage wheels, keeping wagons such as these in good repair. Milk was cooled in icehouses and tasted fresh, even on summer days such as these. *Courtesy Lansing Historical Association.*

Oscar Baker of the Town of Danby is shown tending his sheep on his Nelson Road homestead in the late 1890s. The pasture appears to be surrounded by locust fencing. *Courtesy John Shepardson Sr.*

William J. Ranning is standing in front of his horseshoeing shop on South Street, Dryden, in the early 1900s. An ox is strapped into the shoeing stock or ox sling so its split hooves can be shod. The blacksmith shop remained until the late 1930s, but the site is now the Dryden Police Department parking area. *Courtesy the Nettie Hunt Collection, Dryden Town Historical Society Archives.*

Ralph Space of Millbrook Farm is shown working among his herd of Holstein cows grazing in their summer pasture off McClintock Road, Dryden. Cows only eat grasses, so progressive farmers kept mustard, burdocks and other weeds mowed down. Beam Hill is in the background. *Courtesy the Eleanor Hammond Collection, Dryden Town Historical Society Archive.*

Frank Moore is shown demonstrating a Lanning, Moore & Son plow at the Trumansburg Fair in the Town of Ulysses in 1918. The agricultural fair provided an opportunity for showing new equipment. These plows were manufactured in Trumansburg. *Courtesy Ulysses Historical Society, FA155.*

Edsall's Saw Mill was one of the many logging establishments scattered around the county at the turn of the twentieth century. There is little known about it. *Courtesy Anna Tichnor's Album, Freeville Village Collection.*

Fred Traver is shown seated on his father's McCormick binder, pulled by a team of oxen, the first to be used in South Danby. His father, Dewitt Traver, is standing by as they cut oats at the Traver Farm on the Fisher Settlement Road. At one time, Dewitt Traver owned eight hundred acres in South Danby. This photograph appeared on the front page of the *Rural New Yorker* magazine. Ken Traver still resides on a portion of the old Traver Homestead. *Courtesy Ken Traver.*

This image, taken about 1915, shows Mrs. Charles F. Cole feeding her chickens in the barnyard of the fifty-acre farm in Dryden. Universally, "egg money" or "pin money" was considered to belong to the woman for her private use. Most farm wives either sold eggs to neighbors or traded their surplus eggs for credit at the local general store. *Courtesy the Nettie Hunt Collection, Dryden Town Historical Society Archives.*

The McClintock-Bruno barn is located on McClintock Road in Dryden. This one-hundred- by forty-foot, six-bay barn's interior steel framing was manufactured and constructed by the Groton Bridge Company in 1907–8. An interior steel bridge, running north–south along the center bay, forms the loft. It was said that the cost of the barn was $4,000 and that the profit to the Groton Bridge Company was $50. *Courtesy The History Center in Tompkins County.*

Presented here are two views of Nettie Thomas Hunt (1876–1955). In one she is shown hoeing her vegetable garden in 1918. In the other she holds her yellow cat, her chicken flock in the background on the family's 150-acre farm located between Beam Hill and Dryden. This farm is now the site of Bridle Lane, Crystal Drive and Catherine Drive, just outside Dryden Village off Harford Road (New York State Route 38). *Courtesy the Nettie Hunt Collection, donated by Calvin T. Hunt, Dryden Town Historical Society Archives.*

Robert "Rob" Wightman worked for the Higgins family for many years. He was very handy with tools and an excellent horseman. He built sleds, milk carts and many small items for the Higginses' farm. He was the only one who could deal with the stallion, Freemont, when he was hitched to farm machinery. *Courtesy People in Caroline Album, Caroline Historical Room.*

The two-man crosscut saw was used to cut logs into blocks that could then be split and used for fuel. Large logs were used for timber, but smaller trees were cut and used to make necessary tools, shingles or, in this case, a "renewable" fuel source. Forest Rello, on the right, is shown in this picture taken April 1907 in Brooktondale, probably on the Lounsbery farm. *Courtesy Lounsbery Album, Town of Caroline Historical Room.*

Forest Rello, shown with his axe, split blocks for a winter's supply of wood, a necessary activity in order to keep a family warm. The photograph was taken in April 1907 in Brooktondale, probably on the Lounsbery farm. *Courtesy Lounsbery Album, Town of Caroline Historical Room.*

Monroe House sits atop his tractor with his daughter, Jean, at their 1071 Michigan Hollow Road farm in Danby, about 1937. Monroe was a lifelong resident of Danby and North Spencer. *Courtesy Jean House Card.*

Willard Van Liew, seated on the left, and Maynard Clark planted cabbages on the Van Liew farm on Van Liew Road, Ulysses. Abram Van Liew can be seen here about 1938 driving his Caterpillar tractor, the first in the area. The cabbages were sold to the Trumansburg sauerkraut factory. *Courtesy Virginia V. Luce.*

Leaving horsepower behind, Alvin and Lee Smith help their father, Leslie, and hired man Bob Westfall load peas aboard a truck on their Groton farm about 1946. Cornell University and the Cooperative Grange League Federation made Tompkins County an agricultural center for the Northeast. *Courtesy The History Center in Tompkins County, 80.130.2626.*

GETTING ABOUT

Getting around Tompkins County has never been easy. Cayuga Lake divides the land. Snow and ice make winter travel unsafe. Rain and mud can render roads impassable in the spring and fall. There are, too, the hills that make travel difficult all year long. In addition to the elements, one had to contend with the quality of the roadway. In Ithaca, some early roads were cobblestone or brick. But early twentieth-century photographs show that many lanes in the county were still unpaved—dusty in the summer and riddled with ruts in rainy and snowy weather. The paved roads of today are products of the 1920s, when improvements were made across America to accommodate that increasingly popular automobile. Before the early macadam roads, stagecoach routes cut by early settlers followed already established Native American trails. Indeed, the initial group of these settlers came to Ithaca on a trail that led north from Owego on the track that has become Route 96. Another early road was the Catskill Turnpike. Chartered in 1804, it ran east to west from Catskill on the Hudson to Bath (in Steuben County) along what is today Route 79. When Henry Ford propelled the mass production of automobiles forward, county residents eagerly embraced the new technology, and road improvements followed. Horse-drawn vehicles were steadily replaced by fragile-looking open cars, which, in turn, gave way to heavier, sleeker models. Yet the internal combustion engine was not the only alternative to raw horsepower. In the 1890s, when Americans embraced a bicycle craze, the county was not immune, and the Morse Chain Factory produced an innovative bicycle chain. The Ithaca Cycling Club was formed in 1892, and to this day county residents have remained fond of getting about using pedal power, now on specially marked bike lanes, despite the elements and the hills.

Leona Smith had her picture taken on Fenner Road in Lake Ridge, Lansing. It was a beautiful June day, and the muddy roads common in spring had finally dried up. A large town, Lansing has six named areas: East Lansing, North Lansing, South Lansing, Ludlowville, Myers and Lake Ridge. At one time, each of these areas had its own post office. *Courtesy Lansing Historical Association.*

Fred Warriner's store in Slaterville was located on the corner of Midline and Slaterville Roads. It had many owners until it was torn down and replaced by a convenience store in the early 1970s. The site was purchased by the Town of Caroline, and the modern store was removed in 2008. A town hall annex—to house offices, the community library and records storage—is currently being erected. When there were several other stores in Slaterville, Warriner's store was known as "the Lower Store," and that name persisted even when the other stores were no longer in operation. *Courtesy Volbrecht Spiral Album, Town of Caroline Historical Room.*

Zetta Space is standing beside Grace Griswold Goodrich, seated in her one-horse phaeton or buggy with its convertible top, about 1915. Grace was the wife of lawyer George E. Goodrich, who wrote the valuable town history *Centennial History of the Town of Dryden, 1797–1897. Gift from Goodrich Family Collection, Dryden Town Historical Society Archives.*

One day in the late 1920s, Ed Monroe's aunt and cousin (names unknown) came to visit the Dorn's home located on Bald Hill Road in the Town of Danby. Visiting for an afternoon or for a period of several weeks was common, although mention of visiting falls off in the 1930s. *Courtesy the Monroe Collection.*

The man and woman pictured in the cutter are believed to be Frank and Sarah Higgins of Caroline hamlet. After the town pathmaster had rallied the local men to pack the snow on the Catskill Turnpike, now Slaterville Road, the trip between Slaterville and the hamlet would have taken only forty-five minutes in this open cutter. Since most roads in the countryside were not paved, and moving on snow or frozen ground was easier, people were often able to travel with ease in winter. *Courtesy People in Caroline Album, Town of Caroline Historical Room.*

Earl Trapp (1878–1965), a salesman for the early Maxwell Car Company, is shown demonstrating a "horse-less carriage" on the Church Green at Dryden's four corners in the winter of 1910. Behind him are the original wooden Presbyterian Church, which burned down in late 1938; the Albright Memorial Fountain that was later scrapped during World War II; the church horse and wagon sheds; and the original village bandstand. *Gift of Stella Trapp, Dryden Town Historical Society Archives.*

Heading north on Main Street and passing Spring Street is a group of men in their horseless carriage. The brick building shown in the background was once the Groton Carriage Company and in 1916–17 became part of the Corona Typewriter Company. *Courtesy Rosemarie Palmer Tucker.*

Mr. and Mrs. Fred Atwater and her mother and father, Mr. and Mrs. Charles A. Smith, in front of the Smith home on 121 West Court Street in Ithaca. This twentieth-century image reminds us that the earliest automobiles were a luxury. Fred Atwater founded Atwater's Grocery business, a prosperous grocery store on East State Street in Ithaca. *Courtesy The History Center in Tompkins County, GPF B1.30.*

Frank and Sarah Krum Higgins were farmers in Caroline hamlet. Located at 3262 Slaterville Road, their farm is still owned and operated by family members. This photo was taken before 1903, when a carriage block and concrete sidewalk were built from the front porch to the driveway. The carriage block was a raised platform used to assist entry from the house into a wagon, buggy or other vehicle, making it easier for women in long skirts to step across from the block and into a vehicle than to climb up into one. *Courtesy Higgins Album, Town of Caroline Historical Room.*

Billy Culver sports his haircut while driving his vintage touring car and puffing a "see-gar" in front of the Southworth Library on West Main Street, Dryden, about 1935. This strange haircut, shaven with a Mohawk-style topper, was given to him by barbers Art Hines and Joe Cartledge. From the early 1930s, Hines's barbershop was located on the right side of the brick building at 1 West Main Street. It is known that Mabel Lormor was the only woman allowed inside this male domain, where she also got her men's-style haircut. The Grand Union Grocery was on the left side of the building and is now home to the Dryden Community Cafe. *Courtesy Dryden Town Historical Society Archives.*

Members of the Ithaca Cycle Club pose with their bicycles on West State Street in Ithaca. The club was founded in the early 1890s by a group of prosperous Ithacans who celebrated their cycling efforts with annual banquets, offering elaborate menus and humorous programs. This image of the group at the start of a "Century Run," a one-hundred-mile ride around Cayuga Lake, may have been taken in 1900. *Courtesy The History Center in Tompkins County, GPF D1.22.*

Robert Hyde L. Speed and his son John, known as Jack, are shown in the family car in front of their home in Slaterville Springs about 1912. Later in life, Jack was the postmaster in Slaterville and was known for his cigars and wonderful tenor voice. The Speed family came to the town of Caroline in 1805 from Virginia, and many of their descendants are still living in the area. *Courtesy People in Caroline Album, Town of Caroline Historical Room.*

This 1916 Buick Touring Car is parked in front of the home of Henry St. John, at the corner of Cayuga and Seneca Streets in Ithaca. St. John, a public-spirited civil engineer and businessman and Ithaca's first superintendent of public works, was elected mayor of Ithaca in 1891. It was not unusual to see female drivers in the early years of the twentieth century. *Courtesy The History Center in Tompkins County, GPF B1.63.*

A carriage builder by trade, James G. Pritchard's carriages and wagons first appeared in Ithaca in 1890. Recognizing the opportunity to join the rapidly expanding automobile market, in 1915, Pritchard became one of Ithaca's first automobile dealers. This 1916 photo shows several of Buick's earliest models in front of the Pritchard & Son building at 108 West Green Street. In 1926, the family moved their business to South Cayuga Street. *Courtesy The History Center in Tompkins County, GPF B1.99.*

Shown astride his new machine is Ralph Chatfield at the family farm on New York State Route 13, just past Yellow Barn Road. Riding coat, leather leg spats, high-cuffed leather driving gloves and goggles complete his flashy outfit for a fast ride over unpaved country roads on his Indian Motorcycle, about 1915. The bulb horn was used to scare the chickens out of his way and to warn the horses. *Gift of Charles Bernheim, Dryden Town Historical Society Archives.*

Employees of the Ithaca Sand & Supply are pictured loading their truck. Sand & Supply was located at 409 Lake Street in Ithaca, and its president was E.D. Button. This undated image may have been taken in the very early years of the twentieth century. Note the uncovered cab for the driver. *Courtesy The History Center in Tompkins County, GPF B1.49.*

Tex Marshall, a test pilot for Ithaca's Thomas-Morse Aviation during World War I, is shown here at the wheel of his sports car. As a test pilot in an era of new and highly dangerous aviation technology, Marshall was a man of great daring. *Courtesy The History Center in Tompkins County, GPF B1.44.*

This picture shows the Hulse Smith family in the 1920s on their way to pick huckleberries on Connecticut Hill. The Smith family farms, dating from the early 1800s, were located in the southwest corner of Enfield on Connecticut Hill and Black Oak Corners. Hulse Smith is the driver, alongside his wife Mary Goodfellow, their twin daughters Alice and Aline Smith (born 1914), Ella (born 1910) and Ruth Smith Place, Hulse's sister (1897–1984), known in Enfield for her woven coverlets and rag rugs. *Courtesy Town of Enfield historian.*

Frank Martin owned a shop at the corner of Cayuga and Green Streets in Ithaca—Cummings & Martin, Bicycles, Motor Cycles, and Sundries—that first opened in 1909. Martin is pictured here on what was an early motorized bicycle. *Courtesy The History Center in Tompkins County, GPF D1.23.*

Sam Dayhart, a clerk at Rothschild's Department Store and also its first delivery truck driver, strikes a jaunty pose on the running board of his truck, while his helper, Frank Kerrsin, stands in front. They are parked on North Aurora Street in front of the Greek-American Fruit Company, later known as the Ithaca Grocery and Fruit Company. Owned by James Neferis, it was one of Ithaca's first Greek-owned businesses. *Courtesy The History Center in Tompkins County, GPF B1.114.*

In Trumansburg, in 1927 on July 4, the first-prize float in the annual parade (the prize: one barrel of flour) depicted the settling of Shin Hollow. On the left is Charles Clapp, next to Robert McLallen, descendant of John McLallen, who arrived with his brother-in-law, Abner Treman, in 1793. The area became known as Shin Hollow because men, leaving the taverns in the village's earliest days, hit their shins on tree stumps left in the roadway. Photograph by Earl Dean, owner of the truck and third member of the trio. *Courtesy Nancy Dean.*

In this October 5, 1931 photo, mail carriers Jack Gale, Milton Peck, George Gardner, Bert Payne and Donald Cutter are shown posing by their cars, which display signs reading "U.S. MAIL—NO RIDERS." The post office was located in the Newfield Masonic Temple. Cornelius Sebring, an early Newfield settler, became the first postmaster, bringing mail once a week on horseback. In 1902, inauguration of rural free delivery was instituted. *Courtesy Newfield Post Office.*

The D.B. Stewart & Co. Wholesale Grocers delivery truck sits in front of Ithaca's Star Theatre at 119 East Seneca Street in the early 1920s. D.B. Stewart & Co. was a grocery, confectionery and cigar store operating from the 1860s into the early twentieth century. Stewart was involved in local politics as well as commerce: he was the last president of the Village of Ithaca and the first mayor of the City of Ithaca when Ithaca became a city in 1888. *Courtesy The History Center in Tompkins County, GPF B1.52.*

Brian Nevin poses in 1948 with the first car he owned, a 1940 Pontiac. Nevin, a Cornell student at the time, became a well-known antiques dealer in Ithaca and partner of C. Sherwood Southwick. They operated Brianwood Antiques located on West State Street for many years. *Courtesy The History Center in Tompkins County, GPF B1.101.*

Lee Tripp's Gas Station in the center of the village of Dryden is now Time Square Park, with its large clock. The original bandstand on the Church Green and both churches can be seen in this photograph. Note the majestic elm tree, one of many that lined the streets before the Dutch elm disease killed them in the late 1950s. In 1957, chances were sold to win this replica of Amos Sweet's 1797 cabin, home of the six-member Amos Sweet family, first settlers in the Town of Dryden. The original cabin was located at 19 East Main Street on the left side and in the early 1800s was used as the first schoolhouse. *Ross Sherman Collection, Dryden Town Historical Society Archives.*

In 1962, Cliff Holden took this picture of the new Alameda-Lansing Rescue Ambulance. The squad was named for a thirteen-year-old girl, Alameda Goodrich, who had perished in a house fire in Ludlowville in May 1915. When it was decided to create a fire department in Ludlowville, it was named for Alameda. The rescue program of the fire department was added in the early 1950s. *Left to right*: Jerry Stockton, Paul Welch, Jack Burling, Russell Lane, Levi "Red" Wood, Harold "Shorty" Howell, Norman Hoffman and Leo Teeter. *Courtesy Lansing Historical Association.*

LEISURE

At the turn of the twentieth century, people worked hard, but they also made time for leisure activities. They danced until early in the morning and depended on the horse to take them home. Skating and sleighing in the winter and picnics and camping in the summer continued to be favorite outdoor activities especially after the coming of the automobile. There has always been boating and fishing on Cayuga Lake and along its many streams and creeks. Young bachelors formed clubs with odd names, such as the Spit and Whittle Club.

Old Home Days and the Fourth of July were sure to feature a parade with floats and the local village band. Patriotism was festive and celebrated with American flags and bunting-decorated buildings, a time when children draped their bicycles in crepe paper bunting to ride along the parade route. On Memorial Day, schoolchildren waved tiny flags.

Families enjoyed picnic lunches as they sat on the grass to watch their baseball team compete with neighboring clubs. Small teams from the hamlets competed with one another, while the *Post Standard* league supported the teams from industries such as Cayuga Rock Salt. Card games and checkers were played at the local store or during an evening visit with the neighbors. During the Great Depression, children and families played Monopoly, Chinese checkers, Sorry and other board games. Women met in the afternoons to quilt or educate themselves in "Study Clubs."

Television and the Internet now take the place of radio shows, but people still go camping, boating, fishing and visiting in Tompkins County.

The Skilton family camp was located at Crowbar Point on Cayuga Lake. This is an undated picture, probably from the 1880s. Camping along Cayuga Lake has always been a popular activity. The Skiltons were related to the Cooper family, original settlers of Jacksonville. *Courtesy Town of Ulysses Image Box 1.*

In 1876, the Cornell crew team won a triple victory at the Intercollegiate Rowing Association Regalia at Saratoga. Credit for the victory is often given to John Ostrom, the team's captain, stroke, trainer and coach. Ostrom, who rowed from 1873 to 1877, revised the stroke and improved methods of training and the design of the boats used. Cornell University rowing began in 1873. *Courtesy The History Center in Tompkins County, GPF N25.15.*

This picture, taken in 1890, shows the crowd in front of the old Ludlowville Hotel celebrating the Fourth of July. There would probably have been a parade and ice cream for sale. Seated in the foreground are Mr. and Mrs. John Bonta and their grandchildren, Eltha and Yula Gittford. Beautiful hats and formal dress belied the heat of the day. Ludlowville was the largest hamlet in Lansing, and people came in from the outlying areas to swell the crowd for such celebrations. *Courtesy Lansing Historical Association.*

A group of people is pictured boating along the Cayuga Inlet in the early 1900s. In the nineteenth century, the inlet was vital for commercial access to Cayuga Lake and served as a significant connector to the Erie Canal, useful for transshipment of goods brought to Ithaca by rail heading for Buffalo and points west. By the twentieth century, the inlet was mainly used for recreational activities. *Courtesy The History Center in Tompkins County, GPF N25.13.*

Anna Kozel Moravec is shown feeding her pet crow and cat at the Kozel family farm on the Asbury Road, one mile north of the West Dryden Road intersection in the Town of Dryden. The Kozels owned a small dairy farm. Anna currently lives at Longview, an adult residential community on Ithaca's South Hill. *Courtesy Jim and Linda Moravec.*

In 1866, Alonzo and Elizabeth Rumsey of Enfield, along with William Bogardus of Ithaca, went into the broom-making business. The *Ithaca Journal* reported in 1906 that Elmer and Alonzo Rumsey were turning out a large number of brooms each week from their shop, using broomcorn from their own fields. In 1922, their barn and house, located on Woodard Road, burned down, ending all local production of brooms. *Courtesy Town of Enfield historian.*

In 1894, this band was formed and named for its sponsor, the Lansing Elm Grove Inn, now known as Rogue's Harbor. The band is shown here at the Hotel Frontenac across the lake, probably having arrived by steamboat with a group of summer revelers. Years ago, when Patsy Conway led the Ithaca Band, Will Miller persuaded him to visit Lansing to drill the band. The band members had to buy their own instruments and uniforms, and Mr. Conway thought so poorly of the big bass horn that he provided the band with one of his own. *Courtesy Lansing Historical Association.*

Emil and Bill Makarainen, in 1922, shown sparring at the family farm on Comfort Road in Danby. Emil boxed professionally for one year at various venues, including at Stewart Park and in Trumansburg. *Courtesy Makarainen Family.*

A group of families is pictured here pleasure boating about 1910. In the early 1900s, both Ithaca and Cayuga Lake gained in popularity as the lake, waterfalls and the glens attracted people to the area for recreational activities, especially walking. There were increasing numbers of sailboats, steam yachts, campers and visitors (some even renting summer homes) to the lake and surrounding areas. *Courtesy The History Center in Tompkins County, GPF N8.43.*

In the past, winters were cold enough to make ice sailing a common sport on Cayuga Lake. The winter of 1912 was so severe that the entire lake was reported frozen from end to end. Floyd Newman, a Cornell student in 1912, skated with friends from Ithaca all the way up to Cayuga at the northern end of the lake one cold February day. They wisely took the train home that night. *Courtesy The History Center in Tompkins County, GPF P5.31.*

The wedding supper of Leonard Hasewan and Elosia Fish was celebrated by the Reverend Humphreys August 1, 1910. The ceremony took place in Ludlowville and was followed by refreshments under the tent on the lawn. It was quite a large party for those times. *Courtesy Lansing Historical Association.*

In 1908, the Independence Day parade in Slaterville Springs featured the "Merry Widow," a float depicting the idea of "getting the cart before the horse," meaning living with someone without the benefit of marriage. A news article in the *Ithaca Daily Journal* mentioned that "at Slaterville Springs a crowd estimated at 3,000 gathered to enjoy the celebration of the 4th of July, starting with a fantastic parade." There were several running events, a baseball game and interesting trapshooting. Other participants included the Ithaca Colored Band and the leaders of the town government riding white horses. *Courtesy Higgins Album, Town of Caroline Historical Room.*

This photograph shows Margaret Burlingame, Alice Lee Ellis, Pauline Howe, Meredith Lamont and the hair bow worn by Alice Foster. Probably taken about 1910 at the eighty-five-acre A.D. Burlingame farm on the corner of North Street in Dryden, where it connects with the Freeville Road (New York State Routes 13 and 38). It is now the site of the Dryden Queen Diner and Stafford Chevrolet. *Courtesy the Nettie Hunt Collection, Dryden Town Historical Society Archives.*

A parade was a common form of community entertainment in the early years of the twentieth century. This 1904 image of a parade on the 200 block of East State Street in Ithaca displays more than just the colorful marchers. Local stores are shown, and some, like Bool's Florists, still do business in Ithaca today. *Courtesy The History Center in Tompkins County, GPF S15.69.*

This view, taken early in the twentieth century, shows local Etna people gathered in the summertime at Fall Creek, Etna, near the dam. There they waded, swam and boated, and picnicked on the banks of Fall Creek. Note the fashionable swimsuit on the girl preparing to dive off the bow of the boat. *Gift of Judy Auble and Saino Zazzara, Etna Community Association Archives.*

This parade during the 1930s shows young girls watching those who had dressed up. The man on horseback led the Newfield Cornet Band down Main Street passing in front of the present-day Newfield Public Library. The lack of spectators and lines of cars indicate that the parade just started. Today, parades follow the same route ending at the Newfield Central School grounds. *Courtesy the Collection Archives Alive Newfield Public Library and Newfield Historical Society.*

Catherine and Gustav Hilker (left) and Elbert and Ada Schooley (right), parents of Eldon Hilker and Grace Schooley Hilker, spent Friday nights playing the card game Five Hundred at the Hilker residence on Coddington Road, Town of Caroline. On the wall hangs the wedding picture of Gustav and Catherine, who were married about 1897. *Courtesy Terry Hilker Donlick.*

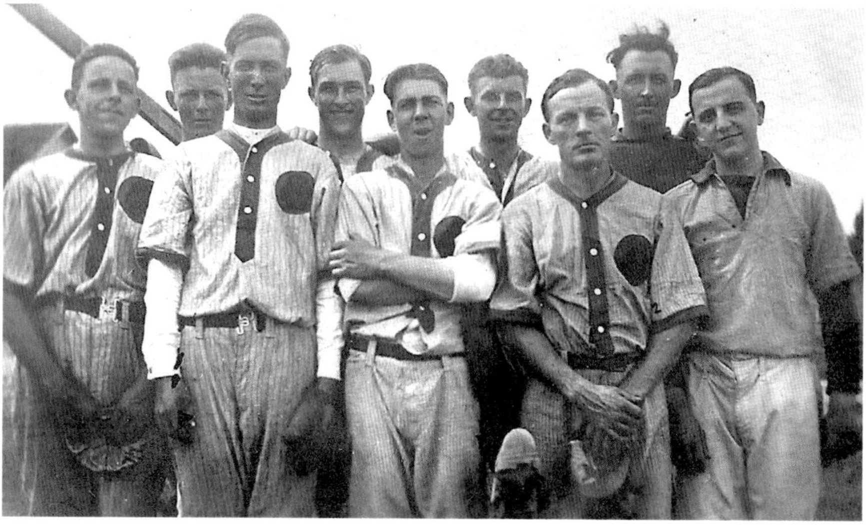

This picture is of the Redmen baseball team of Danby, in 1922. The Redmen was a fraternal organization that owned a hall located on the Danby Road in the center of the Town of Danby where it held dances and card-playing parties. The Redmen Hall was where the general store, which is no longer open, was located. The members of the organization played ball on the field located behind the Danby Town Hall. *Courtesy Sue Thompson.*

This photograph shows a lively group of musicians marching down South Main Street in the Town of Groton in the 1930s. Note the cheerful drum majorette. *Courtesy Rosemarie Palmer Tucker.*

Started in 1931, the annual Mutt Dog Parade brought together neighboring towns of Tompkins County for a day of contests, canines and fun. Presented by Rothschild's Department Store, the Mutt Dog Parade offered prizes for best all-around dog and best out-of-town dog. Leisure activities like these were common Depression-era diversions. *Courtesy The History Center in Tompkins County, GPF S15.197.*

Saturday night street dances were free to all and drew large crowds, quickly becoming a Trumansburg Village tradition. Shown here, from left, are Art Furcha, Hattie Kimple Beardsley, Ted Pearsall, Ed Parkhurst and Pop Kelly, the caller. *Courtesy Town of Ulysses, Box 5.*

Robert H. Treman State Park was originally called Enfield Glen. This 387-acre parcel was donated to New York State in 1921 by Robert H. and Laura Treman. The lower part of the park is used for camping and swimming. The park now totals 1,070 acres. *Courtesy New York State Office of Parks, Recreation and Historic Preservation, Finger Lakes Region, 306 West King Road, Ithaca, New York, 14850.*

William A. Myers of Freeville with a group of local sportsmen trapshooting, still a popular sport. This photo was taken about 1930. *Courtesy Joan Manning.*

Swimmers wave for the camera at Beebe Lake on the Cornell campus. The lake was created in the late 1830s when Ezra Cornell dammed Fall Creek. The dam was later replaced with a new one when the university built its hydraulic laboratory at Triphammer Falls. This undated picture was probably taken in the 1920s, as suggested by the style of bathing suits shown on the male swimmers. *Courtesy The History Center in Tompkins County, GPF C20.17.*

Fred D. Rumsey (1870–1967) was a very active member of the Enfield and Tompkins County agriculture community. His family farm was located at Trumbulls Corners, Newfield. He had been involved both in official and exhibitor capacities in the Tompkins County Fair since 1884 and was an active member of the Enfield Valley Grange for over sixty-three years. This posed photo from the 1950s was intended to be used for one of the many civic organizations that he belonged to in the community. *Courtesy Town of Enfield historian.*

Known throughout Ithaca for his cheerful nature and familiar whistle, Carl Black, who was born with cerebral palsy, is pictured here in 1950 with Donald Robinson and Kathie Kohles near his home on Titus Avenue. With the help of the local Cerebral Palsy Association, Black was given a bicycle specifically designed for people with disabilities with an additional attachment of a refrigerator box, used to sell his "Blackie" ice cream and popsicles. *Courtesy The History Center in Tompkins County, Curt Forester, 80.130.889.*

In the 1930s, Janet McKinley Bradley and friends sailed her Comet Class boat in a gentle breeze along the shore of Cayuga Lake. Laser Class boats made of Fiberglas have superseded the Comet Class. In former days, the lake was used as a highway for commercial activity, but by the mid-twentieth century it had become more of a recreational playground. *Courtesy Lansing Historical Association.*

CHILDREN AT SCHOOL

Two seats of higher education rise up on the heights over Cayuga Lake and give Tompkins County a learned tone. Cornell University and Ithaca College might command the high ground and much attention today, but since 1795 parents and state government allocated money to provide youth with classrooms, educate them in the basics and encourage them to strive for more. For their part, the students have gone off to school and have reveled in their courses of instruction, the chance to engage in extracurricular activities and sports, and the opportunity to meet others of their age and to form friendships. Some youth, of course, went to school grudgingly; the 1874 Public School Law made their attendance compulsory until the age of sixteen. That same law also gave us the basic structure of school organization that led to the system we have today, with six school districts covering county. Their creation led to the demise of the one-room schoolhouses across the county—the last closed in the 1950s—as consolidated elementary and high schools arose. The intimacy of the small community schools, still to be glimpsed at events in the Eight Square School House in the Town of Dryden, was replaced with larger numbers of academic classes, team sports, school dances and school colors. After graduation, county youth aspire to study at Cornell University (founded in 1865 and opened in 1868), Ithaca College (founded in the City of Ithaca in 1892 as the Ithaca Conservatory of Music and then moved to South Hill in 1960) and Tompkins Cortland Community College (founded in 1969 in the Town of Groton and then moved to the Town of Dryden in 1974).

Neighbors Eva Goodrich, Nellie McKee and little Milo Goodrich are enjoying a late winter snowfall in April 1894, at a time when boys and girls up to the age of six wore the same clothes. The house, originally in the Greek Revival style, is located at the corner of South and Union Streets. In 1884, William Henry Miller designed an addition to create the Southworth Library. Ten years later, the current Southworth Library, also designed by Miller, was built. *Gift of Van Sickle Family, Dryden Town Historical Society Archives.*

Ithaca students worked in the garden on the corner of North Cayuga and Jay Streets in 1907. Teachers often used the outdoors as a tool for learning. By the early 1890s, this became known as nature study. Renowned Cornell horticulturist Liberty Hyde Bailey developed a series, *Rural School Leaflets*, which provided teachers with ideas for connecting their pupils to the world around them. Bailey wrote, "One plant cannot be handled without leaving an impress on the life." *Courtesy The History Center in Tompkins County, GPF V30.51.*

Taken before 1920, this photograph shows a football game during recess at the Willow Creek School, District 11 in the Town of Ulysses. The building, at the intersection of Willow Creek and Agard Roads, was later renovated into an apartment house. *Courtesy Ulysses Historical Society, Fred Beardsley Album.*

Shown in this picture are high school students in a science laboratory at Freeville High School on November 14, 1914. The school was located on Main Street and closed in 1936. *From left:* Jerome Davis, Fay Catanch, Frank Snyder, Edgar Dickens, "Professor" Bigelow, Virona Simons and Florence Cole. *Courtesy Joan Manning.*

Students are wrapped in blankets against the chilly air of open windows at Ithaca's Open Air School, 1919. Founded in 1917, this innovative program accommodated children who had health problems, including tuberculosis, malnourishment and heart problems. It offered special nourishment and rest periods in the open air. Classrooms initially were kept at a chilly sixty degrees throughout the year but were eventually raised to seventy degrees. Later called the Health School, it closed in 1948. *Courtesy The History Center in Tompkins County, GPF V25.105.*

J. Paul Munson taught and was principal at the Ludlowville School from 1917 to 1920. He later became superintendent of the Lansing School System, a job he held for thirty-seven years. Munson was educated in a one-room school in Lansing and graduated from Cortland High School and Oberlin College, from which he received a degree in 1913. While teaching at the American University in Beirut, Lebanon, he met and married Johanna Huffnagel, a native of Holland, who taught French and German at the university. *Courtesy Lansing Historical Association.*

Orchestra practice took place in the open air at Ithaca High School in this 1928 photograph. The terrace was used for many education activities at the downtown school, including open-air rest periods for the Health School students. The building is now the DeWitt Mall. Ithaca's current high school opened in 1960. *Courtesy The History Center in Tompkins County, GPF V25.47.*

The Ithaca High School cross-country team poses for a photo after the 1927 season. Coached by Mr. Royal Gilkey (on the right), the boys enjoyed a successful season, in which two of its runners qualified for the state meet in Troy, New York. Unfortunately, many of the larger schools in the section discontinued their cross-country programs around this time; thereafter it was difficult for Manager Herson to create a competitive schedule for the team. *Courtesy The History Center in Tompkins County, GPF V25.38.*

A Tom Thumb wedding staged by the members of Villa Myers's class in Freeville in 1927. These ceremonies were a fad during the 1920s, featuring children under the age of ten. The mock ceremony refers to the actual wedding in 1863 of General Tom Thumb (born Charles Stratton) to Lavinia Warren, who toured with P.T. Barnum. Barnum managed the general's career onstage. *Courtesy Myers-Manning Collection.*

Students at the East Lawn School are pictured here in 1933. The school, opened in 1825, was one of Ithaca's earliest. East Lawn was located on Mitchell Street and closed during district consolidation in 1956. *Courtesy The History Center in Tompkins County, GPF V25.97.*

This classroom was located to the right on the main floor of Freeville High School. This photo was taken on June 1, 1930. The teacher, Beatrice Edsall standing near the back doorway, was a longtime Freeville resident and a member of the school staff for many years. *Courtesy Joan Manning.*

The Baker girls are shown climbing Bald Hill Road on their way to school at the North Bald Hill School in September 1935. This was Joyce's first day of school. *From left*: Joyce, Irene, Edith and Helen Baker. *Courtesy Edith Baker-Waugh.*

Farms were the topic of this unit taught in the Sight Saving room of Ithaca's Health School, shown in this photo from the 1938–39 school year. This room was specially set up with hundreds of fifty-watt light bulbs for students with vision problems. Older pupils were taught to type, and special textbooks were printed for them in large typeface. *Courtesy The History Center in Tompkins County, GPF V25.112.*

First graders at Henry St. John School posed for the camera in June 1940. The school served children from the southwest side of Ithaca until it was closed in 1983. Despite the concern of some Ithaca families, five district schools closed that year: St. John, East Hill, West Hill, Danby and Glenwood Schools. *Courtesy The History Center in Tompkins County, GPF V25.9.*

One of the one-room district schools in Lansing was District 9 in Ludlowville, which by the 1930s had combined to become an elementary and secondary school. After completing grade eight in one of the small one-room schools, students could choose to attend high school in Ludlowville, Ithaca, Groton or King Ferry, their tuition paid by the district. In 1948, all district schools were consolidated into the Lansing Central School District. *Courtesy Lansing Historical Association.*

From left: Trumansburg Central School band members Dean Madison, Janeen Lane, Doris Gottberg Corbin and Catherine Burns Stover are seen headed to march in a parade along West Main Street in 1946–47. Edward Hamill, the band director, taught for many years. *Courtesy Ulysses Historical Society.*

This one-room school is now a small private home on East Shore Drive. The number of students in these small schools varied from year to year, and often not all the grade levels were represented. The teacher taught in ten-minute periods, calling the different classes to the front of the room for their lessons, while the rest of the room was busy with seatwork or helping the younger children with their lessons. Friday afternoons were often devoted to whole school learning experiences. *Courtesy Lansing Historical Association.*

Students line up for the 1946–47 Dryden-Freeville School yearbook photograph in the Shop Building, a two-room building located between the James Street School and Union Street. The art and drafting room was located at one end and the woodworking shop at the other. Shown is the entire shop class: Ken Hoyt with wood drill, Paul Heath, Jake Barnes, Bob Davenport with drawshave and tape and Glen Lasby with saw. Other woodworking tools are mounted on the wall behind them. This was a time before Levi's and blue jeans were worn by anyone other than farmers and cowboys—and before clothing carried any advertising. *Photographed by and from the collection of Elsie Gutchess.*

Groton High School students happily peer from the windows of the school bus. Could it be it the last day of school with summer vacation just beginning or might they just be happy to be seen by the photographer? At the time this picture was taken, school buses were not the bright yellow that we know today. *Courtesy The History Center in Tompkins County.*

The town of Caroline once had twenty-one school districts. When children reached grade seven, they went to high school at Candor, Dryden, Ithaca or Newark Valley. Slaterville School was used as a high school between 1910 and 1914, and students could receive a teaching certificate. When the Ithaca City School District consolidated in 1957, the one-room schools were closed, and children were divided among the Ithaca schools. The Slaterville School was a two-room school and was used until Caroline Elementary School opened in the fall of 1959. Today, Caroline Elementary School is the only school in the town. *First row, front to back*: Shown here with teacher Mrs. Lena Fuller are Doug Nash, Rusty Crispell, Brenda and Bonnie Crispell, John Rueske and Jerry Marion. *Second row, front to back*: Coleene Gee, Mike Nash, Raymond Hines, Helen Burlingame, Carolyn Chillson and Doug Knapp. *Third row, front to back*: Wayne Armstrong, Dave Moesch, Billy Starr, "Tex" Utter, James Stevens and Fred Ink. *Fourth row, front to back*: Charlie Terpening, Larry Utter, Bobby Nash, Kathy Green, Janet Fuller and Jerry Morner. *Courtesy Schools in Caroline Album, Town of Caroline Historical Room.*

Art class in Mrs. Florence Snyder's classroom at the three-room Forest Home School in Ithaca, about 1955. Mrs. Snyder taught a combined first- and second-grade class; art instruction was provided by Cornell University students. The former Forest Home School building, erected in 1921, now serves as the Cornell Plantations' Lewis Building. This photograph was reportedly part of a display at Cornell University's Farm and Home Week. *Courtesy Forest Home Archives.*

Teacher Cecil Casey Keane is seen peeking out of the window. When she began her teaching career, it was not the norm for married women to work outside the home. When her husband was diagnosed with a brain tumor, Cecil Keane became the family breadwinner. This photo includes three of her grandsons and two step-grandsons. *Back row, from left*: Brenda Lawrence, Margaret Zimmer, Robert Mulks, Wesley Zimmer, Howard Golden, Robert White, Bradley Lawrence and Richard Clark. *Second row, from left*: Mable Golden, Barbara Mix, Sandra Durbon, Leah Kobasa, Ronald Clark, James Golden and Ernest Hamilton. *Third row, from left*: Charles Hamilton, John Keane, Kathleen Lawrence, Ellen Nash, Bruce Kobasa and Rose Golden. *Front row, from left*: Walter Hanson, Charles Nichol, Jeff the dog, Roger Keane and Richard White. *Courtesy Schools in Caroline Album, Town of Caroline Historical Room.*

Shown in the 1960s, second graders play on the seesaw at East Hill School. Children on the "up" seesaws are Dianne Dilger, an unidentified girl and Cathy Cook. All of the others are unidentified. East Hill School was located at the corner of Stewart Avenue and State Street and was open from 1881 until 1983, when the district consolidated several schools. *Courtesy The History Center in Tompkins County, GPF V25.81.*

Art teacher Robert Timerson and his students at the Trumansburg Central School are shown at an outdoor painting session sometime in the 1960s. Timerson taught junior and senior high school art for over twenty-five years. *Courtesy Ulysses Historical Society, ED 420.*

In the early 1900s, amateur drama was a popular form of entertainment, and plays were performed in Dudley Hall, Main Street, in Newfield. Here, the Baptist Church's Philathea class of 1917 performs in the play *Aunt Dink's Quilting Party*. *Back row, from left*: _____ Wopot, Mary Tompkins Caslick, Harriet Dickerman, Myrtle Allen, Morton Classen, Willoughby Tucker, George Gardner, Mrs. Bert Smith, Lena Wescott, Clara Sunderlin, Helene Tompkins and Paul Crance. *Front row, from left:* Maude Keene, Iva Tompkins, Leah Classen, Mrs. Dowd, William Dowd, Lottie Puff, Ella Anderson and Hattie Gardner. *Courtesy the Collection Archives Alive Newfield Public Library and Newfield Historical Society.*

In the fall of 1941, the children at the Field School, District 14, in Lansing, enjoyed a Halloween party. Miss Nedrow was their teacher; Joy Fowler Armstrong is the small child at the far right. At age four, she was not yet a student, but she and her mother walked to the school on Peruville Road to attend the party. Joy's brother, Ed, is standing behind her with his hands on her shoulders. The two people in the back without masks are Eleanor Neilson and her brother. *Courtesy Lansing Historical Association.*

Marion Preston Hoagland with her lunchbox, riding in the back of grandfather Harry Givens's truck as he delivered milk cans from his Gee Hill farm to Borden's on South Street, Dryden, and then Marion to the Dryden School on James Street in 1923. *Courtesy Elsie Gutchess.*

CHILDREN AT PLAY

Children's play has changed over time. In the 1700s and early 1800s, children often worked alongside adults and engaged in recreational activities with adults at community gatherings. While the early Victorians thought of play as a way to use up excess energy, by the twentieth century play was widely regarded as an essential part of a child's social development. By the turn of the twentieth century, the concept of childhood as a separate developmental stage, with its own kinds of toys and types of play different from that of adults, had spread from the upper classes to the general population.

Although many children (especially those living on farms or whose parents ran businesses) were expected to work or do chores at home, most attended school, where group play was possible. Schoolchildren played in gendered groups: boys were often boisterous, while girls were thought to be more restrained. Toys popular in the nineteenth century included rolling hoops and beanbags, while marbles and tops were popular by the early twentieth century. Jacks were originally made from the anklebones of sheep, and children later played with buttons, stones and eventually with the familiar molded metal jacks. Team sports with specialized gear, such as baseball, football and later basketball and hockey, gradually replaced the simpler "street" games like tag, blindman's bluff, leapfrog, hide-and-go-seek and duck, duck, goose. Children took advantage of Tompkins County's seasons, playing snow sports in the winter and watersports in the summer.

This popular toboggan slide was erected on the south side of Beebe Lake in 1902. The slide was unbanked, and the trip down it was fast, riders clocked at 48.6 miles per hour as the sled shot out onto the ice of the lake. If the steersman was unskilled, the toboggan tipped over, and although this was considered part of the fun, it could result in serious injury. In 1940, the slide was deemed unsafe and permanently closed. *Courtesy The History Center in Tompkins County, GPF F30.139.*

This is a view of Dryden village boys playing hide-and-seek amid the aging maple trees along West Main Street, just past Mill Street, in the fall of 1907. In the background is the Lacy home that was then owned by Ada Belle Lacy Van Vleet, donor of the chiming Village Clock at Southworth Library. This stately 1828 Federal-style house is now the Candlelight Inn Bed & Breakfast. *Courtesy Verne Morton Collection at The History Center in Tompkins County Historical Society Archives.*

Above: This 1920s photograph is of Mary Goodfellow Smith (left), with her twin daughters Alice and Aline Smith (small girls in the middle wearing bonnets) and Ella (wearing larger bonnet), with Ruth Smith Hulse behind the pan. The children attended District 10, known as the "Little Red School House" or as the Nobles School House. The twins came home at night after school and taught their lessons to their younger brother, Earl. *Courtesy Town of Enfield historian.*

Right: Shown is Margie Mettler at the Fred Mettler Farm on Bald Hill Road about 1916. In the late 1930s, all of the homes on South Bald Hill were bought by the federal government and were subsequently taken down. Today this portion of Bald Hill is state land. *Courtesy Irene Chaffee.*

Becky, with her bobbed Dutch-boy haircut, long stockings and black patent leather Mary Jane shoes, is shown with her tricycle in July 1924 at the driveway entrance to the handsome Southworth home at 14 North Street, Dryden. This brick home, built in 1836 by Thomas Southworth, is still owned by the family. *Gift Rebecca Southworth Simpson, Dryden Town Historical Society Archives.*

Harry Hulbert and Donald Warner are shown about 1926 playing on a bridge over Michigan Creek, behind the Hulbert Farm house on Michigan Hollow Road. Children would stand on one side of the bridge, toss sticks in the creek and then rush to the opposite side of the bridge to watch as they floated by. *Courtesy Nancy Pakkala.*

Three West Dryden children return from a successful fishing trip. Elizabeth Fulkerson holds a stringer of small fish, and Robins Brown and pigtailed Pauline Howe have their homemade fishing poles. The photograph was taken about 1910. *Courtesy the Nettie Hunt Collection, Dryden Town Historical Society Archives.*

Above: Flexible Flyers were popular sleds used by generations of children. Here, about 1910, a smiling and happy Merrit Lamkin is pulled on his sled in front of his home on Shaffer Road by twin bulls, Buck and Brady. Their cowbells let everyone know that they were coming. Merrit died of poliomyelitis at the age of sixteen. *Courtesy the Collection Archives Alive, Newfield Public Library and Newfield Historical Society.*

Left: Here is Calma Hulbert with her "dolly" at the Hulbert Farm on the Michigan Hollow Road in the mid-1920s. *Courtesy Wayne Myers.*

Above: Picture postcards, a popular way of keeping in touch with friends, required only a name and a town for mail delivery. This postcard was addressed to Miss Margaret Dorn, Newfield, New York, from her friend Marcella Simpson and was presented as a "xmas gift altho rather late." A picture of herself and possibly her brother, dressed in spring outfits, shows them sitting in a horse-drawn buggy, which was used well into the 1930s. *Courtesy the Collection Archives Alive, Newfield Public Library and Newfield Historical Society.*

Right: Christina Barber Giles stands with her wheelbarrow at the pump in 1953. This hand pump provided water to the house at 298 Jersey Hill Road in Danby. *Courtesy Priscilla Barber.*

Soap Box Derby competitors are shown here ready to take off down Eastwood Avenue about 1935. Popular among American youth, these gravity-powered racers started on ramps atop hills or on steep streets, making Ithaca an ideal location for this event. The first official All-American Derby was held in Dayton, Ohio, on August 19, 1934. Cities across the country continue to hold their own races with the winners advancing to the finals, still held in Ohio. *Courtesy The History Center in Tompkins County, J25.68.*

James Street, Dryden, neighbors Cal, Larry and Louise Hunt and Eddie McKeon (front) pose in 1939 with their new wagons. In the rear is the Dryden Central School's new addition, containing auditorium, gymnasium and music room. This newly completed building made the famous Spring Concerts possible, held under the direction of music teacher Ola F. Woodward. All three hundred children in the school, from kindergarten to seniors, were involved in this extravaganza, which packed the auditorium to standing room only! *Courtesy the Hunt Family Collection, Dryden Town Historical Society Archives.*

Bernard Hogben shown sledding at the home of his grandparents, Mr. and Mrs. Fred Layen, at 67 Layen Road, Danby, in 1934. Bernard's parents later bought the farm at 379 Gunderman Road, and a good deal of that farmland is still owned by the family. *Courtesy Bernard Hogben.*

On Etna Lane, just off Main Street in Etna, little Frank "Buster" Cogswell, with his homemade bow and arrow, is shown in 1905 walking on the plank sidewalk. The Root Hotel can be seen in the rear. For many years, the Cogswell family ran the general store and post office in Etna. *Gift of Betty Cogswell, Dryden Town Historical Society Archives.*

In this unidentified picture a well-dressed child rides his sturdy tricycle. His trousers are buttoned to his shirtwaist to hold his outfit together. *Courtesy Lansing Historical Association.*

The Lis twins, Stephanie and Stanley, who was called "Ike," lived on the Michigan Hollow Road in the Town of Danby. Their farm is the current site of the Cayuga Lake Beagle Club. The foundation for the barn remains. *Courtesy Helen Dalton-Ed Lis.*

Right: Four little girls can be seen climbing in the tree searching for the biggest apples during the fall of 1939. Highest are Barbara and Marcia Wright, lower are Carolyn and Beverly Berquist—all lived in the first block of East Main Street, Dryden. *Photographed by and courtesy Elsie Gutchess.*

Below: Ithaca's Southside Community Center was a full-service community center under the directorship of James L. Gibbs in the late 1930s and 1940s. Providing job training for adolescents and adults, as well as recreational and educational activities for children, Southside was and still is significant for Ithaca's African American community. In this 1930s picture, children work on art projects. *Courtesy The History Center in Tompkins County, FBO.0015.31.*

Teenagers engaged in professional training, as well as recreational and sports activities, at Ithaca's Southside Community Center. High school students could participate in job training programs, and some were among the first to break the color barrier in Ithaca during the 1940s and 1950s. Here, local students enjoy a game of ping-pong in 1939. *Courtesy The History Center in Tompkins County, FBO.0067.38.*

In 1942, three young girls—Joanne Gutchess, Carleen Brown Skawski and Bertha Lacy La Motte of the Fall Creek Farm Market in Freeville—line up for this photograph after making "dolls" from the hollyhocks growing in the background. The flower buds, or doll's heads, were stuck with toothpicks to the colored blossoms that made the skirt or body. These little figures were used to create tiny scenes or parades. The ground is strewn with the discards. In the background is the Gutchess family Victory Garden with corn, tomatoes, lettuce and more, located to the rear of 12 East Main Street, Dryden. *Photographed by and courtesy Elsie Gutchess.*

Above: Earl Dean photographed two neighbor boys on Park Lane in Jacksonville in 1940. Charles Frazier is on the sled, and Edwin Crumb is standing. *Courtesy Nancy Dean.*

Right: Grace Schooley Hilker enjoying a sunny day with her daughter Terry Hilker at 522½ Seneca Street in the City of Ithaca. In the 1940s, toys were often simple in design such as this push toy with a cylinder between two wooden wheels. Notice Terry's high-top leather, laced shoes and her mother's upswept, fashionable hair. During World War II, it was popular for women to style their hair in Victory rolls and tight curls. *Courtesy Terry Hilker Donlick.*

Children enjoying a pool at 508 East Buffalo Street, Ithaca, in the late 1940s. The little girl on the left is Suzanne Long Palmer, with two friends named Miller. In the rear of the picture are Suzanne's sister, Marcia, and her grandmother, Pearl Morey. *Courtesy Freeville Village Collection.*

Sol Goldberg, who photographed these children in a fountain at Stewart Park, took thousands of images of Ithaca and Cornell. During the time he was a photographer for the *Ithaca Journal* (1956–65), he roamed the Ithaca streets looking for human-interest stories. His work was often offbeat or humorous and always technically competent. *Courtesy The History Center in Tompkins County, 2001.29.1.351.*

Beautifully costumed butterflies gently floated around the stage in *Rhapsody Dance* at the 1939 Spring Concert to entertain the full house audience at the Dryden Freeville Central School auditorium on James Street. *Back row*: Ruth Fulkerson, Helene Kehler and Ida May Marshall. *Middle*: Bettina Heath, Shirley Settle and Geraldine Whittier. *Front*: Dorothy VanArkel, Joyce McKinney and Jane Maughan. *Gift of Joyce McKinney Perkins, Drydenettes Archives.*

The students of Mrs. Helen Avery's second-grade class participate in a maypole dance in the spring of 1963 at Belle Sherman School in Ithaca. Helen Avery taught second grade at East Hill School from 1938 to 1952 and at Belle Sherman from 1952 to 1970. *Courtesy The History Center in Tompkins County, GPF V30.72.*

This unidentified 1950s image shows children playing on a jungle gym in Ithaca. The younger children are being monitored by the older students. *Courtesy The History Center in Tompkins County 80.130.898.*

IN PERIL

Lightning strikes. Floods. Train derailments. Fires. Whether the work of nature or the result of human error, lives, homes and livelihoods are placed in peril by such disastrous events. They can shatter lives and shake communities. When people are at risk and danger is imminent, however, communities also come together. Neighbors help neighbors, and strangers rush in to lend a hand. This had been true in Tompkins County as elsewhere, and the evidence of how disasters bring people together even as things come apart is to be seen in these photographs. In its history, the county has been spared destruction and death of gigantic proportions; Tompkins has seen no flooding on par with the water damage wrought by Hurricane Agnes in Chemung County in 1972, and we have not witnessed a transportation accident of the magnitude of the train wreck in Angola, Erie County, which claimed fifty lives in 1867. Yet residents of Tompkins County have known danger and have acted to meet it. There were the significant floods of 1905, 1922 and 1935; the last of these left eleven dead and the southwest area of Ithaca completely underwater. Numerous homes and prominent buildings have been lost to fire, particularly in the Ithaca fire of 1871. Cars too numerous to count have wrecked, trains and trolleys have leapt their tracks and boats have foundered in the waters of Cayuga Lake. If the toll of those hurt, some mortally, did not warrant attention outside of the county, the risk to life was no less real, and the brave response of those who came to help in the time of need was no less meaningful.

In 1890, floodwaters threatened activities at the Tompkins County Fairgrounds on Elmira Road in Ithaca. Note the flags on display, pitched tents and half-submerged carriages. It was one of several times that the downtown area of Ithaca suffered from flooding. *Courtesy The History Center in Tompkins County, GPF M1.67.*

The Ithaca Athens Railroad, which later became part of the Lehigh Valley Railroad, began in 1871, opening a route from Ithaca to Athens, Pennsylvania, a three-hour journey, with an important stop in East Newfield then called Nina. Train derailments were not uncommon and provided an opportunity for folks to gather, have their picture taken and even picnic. Today, the station at Depot Road in Newfield is closed, and only freight trains pass through. *Courtesy the Collection Archives Alive, Newfield Public Library and Newfield Historical Society.*

Nestled between three hills of the Appalachian uplands, crisscrossed with major creeks and built on the floodplain of Cayuga Lake, Ithaca was prone to flooding. As a result of the massive flooding of 1935, the Army Corps of Engineers built a flood control channel in the 1960s to mitigate the kind of flooding pictured here in this 1901 image. *Courtesy The History Center in Tompkins County, GPF M1.69.*

On October 9, 1907, a barn and two livery stables, located at the corner of West Main and Hector Streets in Trumansburg, burned down, killing two men and seven horses. Liveries provided transportation for the village and from the Taughannock Hotel, across Main Street. *Courtesy Town of Ulysses Box 5 Image Collection.*

Above: This image shows Jack Sincebaugh repairing a hole in the road leading to Ludlowville. This road runs along Salmon Creek gorge, where there were frequent washouts that needed repair. People often refer to this road as the "Snake Road" because of its narrow, twisting way. For a while in the 1990s it was closed to traffic, but because of its convenience for travel to Ludlowville, it has been thoroughly rebuilt. *Courtesy Lansing Historical Association.*

Left: In the early morning of February 14, 1912, a fire completely destroyed the Ithaca High School located on East Buffalo Street and built in 1885 on the school lot first occupied by the coeducational Ithaca Academy (1821). The No. 6 Fire Department used steam pumpers to put out the blaze. Afterward, classes were held in private homes until the new building opened in 1914, in what is today the DeWitt Building. *Photo by Sidney Thompson, courtesy Sue Thompson.*

To make butter in a barrel churn, cream is poured through the top, which needs to be fastened securely. The large crank rotates the barrel end over end. To allow the gas that forms to escape, there is a small hole near the bottom of the barrel that needs to be opened. Failure to remove the cork in time can result in a blowout, with cream spilling all over. In this early twentieth-century picture, Mrs. Dallas King of Ridge Road, Lansing, is seen mopping up the mess. *Courtesy Lansing Historical Association.*

In the late 1920s, the Red and White grocery store in South Lansing caught fire. Bernard Ruzika and Ed Osmun discovered the blaze and woke the owner, George Bardo, who was sleeping in the burning building. Town trucks pulled down the store to keep the fire from spreading. *Courtesy Lansing Historical Society.*

On May 5, 1921, a Morse Chain worker discovered smoke from the paint shop of the Treman King Hardware building located on the corner of East State and South Cayuga Streets in Ithaca. Five fire companies responded to the call, but the flames were so intense that the firemen were forced back one hundred feet. When the blaze was brought under control, only the brick shell of the four-story structure remained. *Courtesy The History Center in Tompkins County, GPF L10.22.*

The flood of 1935 had terrible consequences for the county. Roads around the county were closed for several days, including Brooklyn Road, near Fall Creek, in the Village of Freeville, and flooding caused much damage. Shown here in the midst of water, from left, are Homer Collins; Mildred, Jane and Jean Genung; Raymond Sickmon; and John Collins. *Courtesy the Freeville Village Collection.*

On July 8, 1935, standing knee-deep in floodwater, neighborhood boys on Ithaca's West Buffalo Street, near the railroad tracks, smile with delight. That day, creeks spilled over their banks, destroying city property, and the lake level rose four feet. Ithaca was one of many communities throughout the Northeast that suffered flooding that summer. *Courtesy The History Center in Tompkins County, GPF M1.191.*

Cleanup after the 1935 flood required removing tons of gravel at the foot of West Hill where the Mecklenburg and Trumansburg roads meet. In Tompkins County eleven lives were lost to the rampaging floodwaters, and damage to the Southern Tier counties was estimated at $25 million. *Courtesy The History Center in Tompkins County, GPF M1.250.*

Seven Holstein cows, grouped under a tree for shelter during a downpour in the 1920s were hit by lightning on Charles Pratt's one-hundred-acre farm on the Dryden/Ithaca Road between Springhouse and Johnson Roads in the Town of Dryden. *Courtesy Nettie Hunt Collection, Dryden Town Historical Society Archives.*

An automobile accident on West Main Street, in the Village of Dryden, was the deadliest in the history of the Town of Dryden. On March 10, 1915, an accident took the lives of four members of the Henley Hunter family. Mr. Hunter was a lumberman, and the family had lived on West Main Street. *Gift of Ed and Helen Little, Dryden Town Historical Society Archives.*

A massive snowstorm in January 1945, after the children had been let off at the Dryden Central School, lasted for four days. Two hundred schoolchildren—from Freeville, Etna and McLean—were fed and sheltered for the entire week because all roads were shut. The town dispatched snowplows, but some of them also became stuck. Four days later, a crew of eight with hand shovels and a chain are shown on Irish Settlement Road trying to free the bus and a snowbound plow. *Photograph by Ross Sherman, courtesy Dryden Town Historical Society Archives.*

A&P Foods grocery chain had stores throughout Tompkins County during the middle of the twentieth century. This one, on West State Street in Ithaca, caught fire in February 1940. Firefighters had difficulty dealing with fires in cold upstate New York winters. Hydrants often froze, making water supplies inaccessible. *Courtesy The History Center in Tompkins County, GPF L1.218.*

On August 15, 1947, the intersection of State and Aurora Streets in Ithaca flooded. To the left is the old Ithaca Hotel. *Courtesy The History Center in Tompkins County, GPF M1.282.*

In February 1954, fire damaged the Dryden-Freeville Central School, which was "Up Among the Towering Pine Trees" on James Street. Damage was estimated at $400,000. Eight classrooms and the cafeteria were gutted, and the newer portion of the building, erected in 1936–37, suffered from water and smoke damage, leaving seven hundred students stranded. Instead of adding to the existing building, the board of education bonded to erect a new high school. *Ross Sherman Photograph and Collection, Dryden Town Historical Society Archives.*

West State Street, between Corn and Meadow Streets in the City of Ithaca, was suitable for wading but not for traffic during the 1935 flood. By 1969, construction of the flood control channel at the head of Cayuga Lake ended threats from water in Ithaca's low-lying areas. *Courtesy The History Center in Tompkins County, GPF M1.76.*

In March 1953, a private airplane owned by General Mills, Inc., crashed at Old Main and Bradley Streets in Trumansburg, killing the two men onboard. Local observers included Edwin Brown, far left in coveralls, and Royden Green, front center, standing and not wearing a hat. Russell I. Doig, in the back row center, is wearing a hat. *Courtesy Ulysses Historical Society, ARP 2119.*

IN HARMONY

Most of the images in this book depict activity: people working, playing, riding about, learning or celebrating. Yet there are other important moments in our lives that are defined by the suspension of activity and even of time. These moments happen when we come together in companionship, sorrow, thanksgiving or contemplation. They occur when we engage with others in a shared situation or emotion; they are the instances when we connect with someone else. These are the times that transcend the busyness of our lives; they are the times when our souls are fed by our common sense of humanity.

Pause a minute to consider the connection portrayed in these diverse pictures. Who has not stood at a grave site or sat comfortably in silence with another person? Who has not experienced the pleasure of looking up to see approval in someone's eyes or to note a shared concern? We are all individuals and alone, and yet we grow by the connections we make with others. We experience our own humanity, and it expands as we undergo communion with those with whom we share this planet. What can be as important as the bond created between individuals and with this lovely land on which we live?

This picture shows Henry Speed (1847–1934) on the left and James Webb (1823–1919), descendants of John James Speed, slaveholder from Virginia and early settler in the town of Caroline, and Peter Webb, a former slave who had belonged to J.J. Speed. When Henry Speed rode with the milkman from Slaterville to Caroline to see his friends, he often visited with James Webb. *Courtesy People in Caroline Album, Town of Caroline Historical Room.*

These two women, possibly mother and daughter, take a moment from their knitting to smile for the camera. Their hairstyles, mode of dress with bowties and long aprons to protect their skirts indicate that the time was during the 1890s. Note the fashionable parlor with footrest, yarn stand and intricate carpeting, displaying a rather opulent environment in which these women pursued their handiwork. *Courtesy the Collection Archives Alive, Newfield Public Library and Newfield Historical Society.*

Ithaca High School girls gather to sew the eleventh star on their Roosevelt flag. This photo appeared in the Ithaca school triennial report for the years ending in July 1917, 1918 and 1919. *Courtesy The History Center in Tompkins County, GPF V30.124.*

In September 1910, paused at the grave of Hattie J. Liddington in the Speedsville cemetery are W.H. Liddington and "Irish." The Town of Caroline has twelve cemeteries and fifteen recorded family plots. Descendants of the Liddington family still reside in the Speedsville-Berkshire area. *Courtesy Speedsville Album, Town of Caroline Historical Room.*

This revival choir is seen in the old Morse Chain building in Trumansburg in the fall of 1912. Harley Mosher was the choir director and Ernest Crabill, the preacher. The combined revival was held nightly for one month, sponsored by the Baptist, Methodist and Presbyterian churches, all of which gained new members as a result. *Courtesy Town of Ulysses Loose Picture Box.*

A workcrew at a sawmill near the Charles Miller farm in Enfield takes time out to pose with the tools of their trade. Pictured are Marian Van Loan, Frank Miller, William Bower, W.S. Drummond, Ira Bower, Floyd Miller and an unidentified man possibly with the last name Updike. It must have been a warm sunny day: note the man on the left in the back holding his hat up to shade his face. *Courtesy The History Center in Tompkins County, GPF J15.3.*

In 1931, the Spit and Whittle Club was started by thirteen elderly men who often sat on the store steps to read their mail, exchange news and rest for the walk home. They formed a club, meeting first in 1931 at the Wavle Hotel, during which they visited, played cards and read the paper and their mail. Yearly dues were two dollars to cover the rent, plus seventy cents for electricity. When the hotel was demolished in 1940 (it is now the site of Dryden First National Bank), the forty-five men moved next door and upstairs over member Art Hines's barbers. They disbanded during the 1940s when the stairs became too much for them to climb. *Courtesy Elsie Gutchess.*

Calvary Baptist Church, located on North Albany Street in Ithaca, was founded in 1857 as the Wesleyan Methodist Chapel as a mission chapel sponsored by the St. James African Methodist Episcopal Zion Church on Cleveland Avenue. It became a Baptist church in 1903. In 1926, the Reverend Benjamin H. Payne began a thirty-nine-year career ministering to the needs of his congregation, and this group photograph was probably taken during his tenure. *Courtesy The History Center in Tompkins County, GPF F1.132.*

By midday on February 21, 1930, the thermometer had reached sixty-two degrees. This photograph shows fourteen men in dark suits, white shirts and hats, gathered on the steps on Main Street in the Village of Dryden in front of Earle F. Lupton's Electric, Refrigeration and Radio Store, the Square Deal Grocery and Lupton's Chevrolet Garage, where regular gas was sixteen cents and high-test gas was nineteen cents per gallon. The men include Fred Macey (standing), John Tripp of Union Street, Frank Johnson of Library Street, C.D. Griswold of Union Street, Andy Myers of North Street, Arnold Hopkins, Clinton Trapp, John Fundis of Freeville, Avery Hiles of North Street, Howard Palmer of Virgil Road and Charlie Cotterill. The others are unnamed. *Courtesy the Nettie Hunt Collection, Dryden Town Historical Society Archives.*

Students at Dryden High during the years 1878–98 were joined by alumni from later classes. This 1951 picture was taken at the Dryden Presbyterian Church. *First row, from left*: Eva Green Rolfe, Alice Cole Burlingham, Rose Hubbard Munsey, Stella Trapp, President Harriet Corbin Colwell, Nettie Morgan Beers, May Sandwick Seamans and Nina Wheeler Livermore. *Second row, from left*: Edith Mahan Tripp, Florence Montgomery Southworth, May Swart Brown, Lana Stilwell, Edna Wheeler Lamont and Nellie Baker Howland. *Third row, from left*: Anna Steele Atkinson, Minnie Stanton O'Niel, Fannie Colman Glazier, Sadie Wheeler Hart and guest Mabel Pulling Scofield. *Back row, from left*: Jennie Wheeler Bartholomew, Jennie Little, Olive Coleman Hanna, May Hill, Carrie Elliott Wilkins and Fannie Tripp Webb. One hundred years later, the group changed its name to the Drydenettes—their mission was to donate memorial books to the Southworth Library. *Gift of Ed and Helen Little, Dryden Town Historical Society Archives.*

Rotary members Bill Halland (left), Louis Smith (center) and Fitch Stephens are pictured boating along Cayuga Lake en route to Sheldrake Point. Fitch Stephens was a prominent local lawyer and Ithaca city attorney in the 1920s and 1930s. *Courtesy The History Center in Tompkins County, GPF P5.54.*

Fred Parshall is shown at his farm on Bald Hill Road in Danby with his horses, Topsy and Trixy, about 1935. Farmland on Bald Hill was considered "hardscrabble," as it was not easy to cultivate because of the irregular topography. *Courtesy Wayne Myers.*

A building crew erected the Mantz cottage on Frontenac in Trumansburg in 1937. Nine of Adrian Pearsall's workers shown, from left, are M. Barthod, Fred Asey, Pearsall, Fred Reigle, Alfred Sherwood, C. Green, Bill Asey, Willis Reigle and Ralph Carman. Crewmember Earl Dean took the photograph. *Courtesy Nancy Dean.*

The campground, located at the corner of Cook and Railroad Streets in the Village of Freeville, belongs to the New York Spiritualist Assembly. Its presence was established in Freeville in 1895, after the development of the railway system. The Assembly facilities were also used by the community for picnics, graduation exercises and dances. Several Freeville families have been members of the Assembly. *Courtesy Freeville Village Collection.*

Above: Toddlers Anna Robbins and Patsy Johnson of Ithaca share an affectionate moment. This timeless image was taken more than sixty-five years ago. *Courtesy The History Center in Tompkins County, FBO.0015.69.*

Left: This unidentified but stylishly dressed woman appears to be fascinated by a framed specimen of a butterly. In 1904, Anna Botsford Comstock, a conservationist, illustrator and a leader of the nature study movement, wrote the book *How to Know the Butterflies*, engendering an interest in the study of nature. Anna Comstock was one of the earliest women to teach at Cornell University. *Courtesy the Collection Archives Alive, Newfield Public Library and Newfield Historical Society.*

During the Great Depression of the 1930s, the Reverend Dutton S. Peters and his wife, Martha, began a Mother's Club for overworked local woman from the Town of Enfield. They also sponsored an annual Mother's Camp. The club began with a core of eleven women who went to Lisle, New York, to a hostel called the Happy Valley Homes, for a week's vacation in August 1933. *Courtesy Town of Enfield historian.*

This flower and plant sale was held in Trumansburg about 1943. Shown are Bernice Smith, on the left, and Anna Smith. At the time, Howard Smith owned the propane gas business on Main Street, and Roy Smith ran the Market Basket grocery store. *Courtesy Ulysses Historical Society, BI.*

Dryden Needle Club began during World War I. The yearly dues of fifty cents funded flowers for ill members. Members enjoyed dinners, visited and sewed. They knit caps for hospital newborns and made cancer pads, socks for soldiers, dressings for a leper colony and quilts for the needy or fire victims. Sometimes they "just needled each other," to quote one member. *Back row, from left*: Carrie Snyder, Lulu Crosby, Jennie Kennedy, Lena Ensign and Miriam Fletcher. *Middle row, from left*: Edna Lamont, Emma Morse and Anna Johnson. *Front row, from left*: Edith Tripp and grandson, Mary McFerron, fifty-year member Libbie Brown and Helen Strong. *Gift of Ruth Sweetland, Dryden Town Historical Society Archives.*

Jim and Sally Oltz Heidt and Randy Smith drove and chaperoned teens to Etna on a wintry Saturday night in 1947. Once the room warmed up, the young people danced to 78 rpm records. The evening featured "no food, no drinks, no drugs, no fights, no problems." *Back row, from left*: Dick Boles, Al Bell, Pat Brownell Goodspeed, George O'Connor, June Olds Bell, Marjorie Robinson Morrisey, Jean King Rundall, Eleanor McKinney Monroe, Glen Lasby and Dolores Maxudian Terry. *Middle row, from left*: Sally Oltz Heidt, Jim Heidt, Diana Williams Landis, Ed Caley, Paul Heath, Bob Davenport and Barb Martin Shew. *Middle row, lower, from left*: Imogene Maxudian and Janis Teck. *Standing at far right*: Randy Smith. *Front row, sitting on floor*: Bill Swope, Myrna Carter, Bill Bailey, Jake Barnes, Joan Hance Spaulding and Dave Couch in back of Randy Shew. *Photographed by and courtesy Elsie Gutchess.*

Land in the Town of Newfield is generally unsuitable for grains, but it abounds with orchards. Several baskets were needed by these young people in this 1930s picture to collect all of the fruit from a backyard tree. Today, orchards such as Littletree Orchards flourish in Newfield, providing everyone with the opportunity to pick apples. *Courtesy the Collection Archives Alive, Newfield Public Library and Newfield Historical Society.*

Eugene Williams and his daughter, Etta, of the hamlet of Caroline, contemplate a large pig in a pen. Williams was a respected farmer in the area who worked different farms "on shares," splitting the profits with the owner. As early as 1811, the Caroline Town Board "Resolved, That swine shall not run on the commons." Still pigs ran free so that in 1812 it was "Resolved, That hogs shall not be free commoners." This photo was taken by Sarah Krum Higgins before 1908, when Gene and his wife, Ida Olney Williams, lived and worked on the Wattles farm. *Courtesy Higgins Album, Town of Caroline Historical Room.*

Right: Store clerks Janes Mesmer Fellows and Malloryville resident Charlotte Old are shown before the Red & White grocery store in Freeville in the early 1940s. County shops and post offices declined after the advent of the automobile, which led to greater mobility. Notice the height of the gas pump compared to those of today. The building with the cupola was once the fire station. *Courtesy Freeville Village Collection.*

Below: L.J. Carpenter (left), conductor, and Sid Carr, engineer for the Auburn Short Line Railroad, are shown in front of the train at the Lehigh Valley Railroad Station in Ithaca. This handshake commemorates the last run of the Auburn Short Line in Ithaca in August 1948. Sid Carr looks justly proud of his thirty-seven years of service. *Courtesy The History Center in Tompkins County, 80.130.1091.*

In the late 1950s, the Hilker family gathered to spend a warm Sunday afternoon at Gustav and Catherine Hilker's residence on Coddington Road in the Town of Caroline. In the foreground, Otto Hilker enjoyed a jovial moment with young Liz Hilker, while other family members look on. Seated on the porch chair, Gustav Hilker watched his granddaughter, Terry Hilker, as his son, Henry, completes a woodcarving. *Courtesy Terry Hilker Donlick.*

This photo from the 1950s was taken at the home of Gustav Hilker (back to the camera) located on Coddington Road, town of Caroline. Families frequently gathered for card playing during this era. *Courtesy Terry Hilker Donlick.*

This 1957 photograph shows children in Vicky Knapp's primary Sunday school class at the Jacksonville United Methodist Church, located in the Town of Ulysses. *Courtesy Jacksonville United Methodist Church.*

Elbert and Ada Schooley hosted a family picnic at their residence on Caroline Depot Road in the Town of Caroline in the early 1950s. Lawn furniture rarely existed in rural areas, and families improvised with whatever was handy. Hilker grandchildren Elizabeth, John and Terry (seated on the step stool) enjoyed a lunch of hot dogs and hamburgers. *Courtesy Terry Hilker Donlick.*

Toula Gordon, John Dentes, John Poulos and Paulette Chelekis Kazinsky are shown here in costume for a Greek Independence Day program in Ithaca March 25, 1956, in the City of Ithaca. Greek-American children in Ithaca still dress in traditional costumes for special celebrations. Greek immigrants began to settle in Ithaca at the turn of the twentieth century. *Courtesy The History Center in Tompkins County, GPF M25.85.*

AFTERWORD

The photographs in this book evoke a remarkable nostalgia for the past. At the same time, we recognize universal qualities of life that never change. Swim attire has become dramatically different since the Roaring Twenties, when Cornellians could swim in Beebe Lake. If we no longer swim there, we still love to cool off on hot summer days. The nature of work may evolve, even in one lifetime. Frank Howland of Lansing shifted from blacksmithing to running a grocery store, adapting his profession to suit the times. But whether farming or manufacturing, successful work always brings pride of accomplishment. Childhood appears to be different in one-room schoolhouses, with blackboards and books instead of videos and the Internet. Playtime found children engrossed with different toys, and there was also time for rambling out of doors, but the delight of boys playing hide-and-seek is still the same. Thanks to better warning systems and rescue operations, we can more effectively respond to devastating fires and floods than was possible one hundred years ago. And yet the loss from these perils is no different today.

At first glance, we note what has changed between the time of the photograph and today. When we look again and consider them a bit, we discern what connects this time to the past and our current ways of work and play to those we glimpse in these images.

Common Scenes

For people in this part of the Finger Lakes, life can be an adventure. The photos here show this, whether ice boating in winter or motor boating from

Ithaca to Myers Point in the Town of Lansing in summer. The streets from Trumansburg to Groton may be turned into fairs with parades and dancing. Even work can be an adventure—soaring to the skies by building bridges or airplanes, burrowing deep underground to mine rock salt or creating new realities through the early film industry.

While exploring the images presented in this book, we glimpse intensely personal and yet universal moments: visiting the grave of a wife and mother, or a newborn baby being weighed by a community nurse. We see women knitting or men on the stoops and sidewalks of Dryden on a freakishly warm day in the middle of February. People of all ages are found tilling the soil, joining in community celebrations or supporting their neighbors at a time of crisis.

The exuberance of small-town daily life is captured in a rare candid shot of a Caroline family gathering. We see several generations together—men, women and young girls laughing and relaxed, unaware of the photographer. How can we not be interested in whatever the girls are doing that has caused parents, aunts and uncles to grin with delight? Their careless, infectious joy draws us in, dissolving the decades between then and now.

These images are similar to thousands of others taken between 1870 and 1960. We see rural family reunions and parades of firemen marching in town. There are men working on a railroad or at a construction site, cutting hay or plowing potatoes. Some are seen showing off their shiny new automobiles, their first delivery truck or a town's new ambulance. We also witness a woman in a shiny new buggy, reins in hand, above a handsome horse. She is dressed in a clean white shirtwaist and dark skirt, smiling and confident. And we catch sight of a group of working women from a small-town blanket factory, dressed with dust caps on their heads and scissors pinned to their blouses. There are pictures showing children playing in a schoolyard and lined up in neat rows at their desks. A few pages on we are reminded of the all-too-common dangers of floods, fires and train wrecks. For each image, unique as it is, a nearly identical image can be found for almost any town in New York…or America.

There's a deep feeling of the familiar because these pictures capture much of the essence of American life: small industry, picnics in the park, a day in school, playing with childhood friends, little mishaps and big disasters. The locale and the specificity of place set these images apart, however. These are *our* lakes and gorges, *our* town streets and country farms and, most importantly, *our* people.

What's the Real Story?

The particulars of place and the stories of the people make these photos unique. They tell many stories, but there is so much that they can not express. These are moments captured in time. Sometimes, because the back story is not obvious, we need a guide—or a set of guides. It takes both a picture and a thousand words to tell the whole story of a place. Fortunately, a dedicated team of researchers and historians have filled in the gaps.

Intangible connections of community are present in all aspects of work and play in Tompkins County. Our relationships define us; they are sometimes quite surprising and defy conventional assumptions. The photo of Henry Speed and James Webb, taken about 1910, depicts a relationship between a senior white man and elderly black man. In this image of two old men, seated along with a young cat on a farmhouse step, Henry would have been in his sixties and James a few years shy of his ninetieth birthday. Speed was a descendant of John James Speed, a former Virginia slaveholder who helped found the hamlet of Speedsville in the Town of Caroline. His slave, Peter Webb, bought his freedom in 1818. Almost a century later, these descendants of slave and slaveholder were well known to one another. The image of the two men enjoying a moment of sun is powerfully evocative.

Looking back, without the back story, it can be easy to misunderstand or draw the wrong conclusions. My first impression of the image of "Blackies" Ice Cream, dished out to a small black boy and white girl by an old white man, was well off the mark. I needed the back story, written by a historian, to explain the picture's significance. Only then could I understand the greater aspect of community represented by this picture. The ice cream man, Carl Black, was born with cerebral palsy. By all accounts, he was a cheerful man. Mr. Black was able to support himself thanks to early efforts by the Ithaca community to provide opportunities to the disabled. In July 1950, the local Cerebral Palsy Association supplied him with a bicycle specially designed for his particular needs, fitting it with a cooler for ice cream sales. His delight in bringing joy to young Donald Robinson and Kathie Kohles on that summer day radiates from the picture.

The Pictures Not Taken

Two pathways diverge in the historical record: the moments seen and those not seen; the images in this book and the photographs not taken. For those who work and play in Tompkins County, both sets of memories—

the public and the personal—are equivalent. This book can only capture the experiences of one path, but the other is just as interesting, meaningful and valuable. Why are there so few photographs of the spiritual, political and community activist aspects of our residents? We might regret that these important, yet seemingly unrecorded, activities aren't better represented. This collection is the result of choices made by artists, reporters, family members and, finally, a team of historians. That has made all the difference.

Any historical record is a collection of accidents. The image of Tompkins County presented here is built from chance frozen moments. We rely on coincidences of particular artists and chroniclers who were attracted to this place and who documented daily life. These pictures represent a photographic selection of people, places and events; yet, no photograph was ever meant to be in this book or connected to the other images in the book. Not all photos taken over the years have survived. Therefore, many images were "accidentally preselected" simply by making their way to the collections at historical societies or kept in family collections.

Another of the accidents of the historical record is that many surviving photographs show people enjoying themselves outdoors on sunny summer days. There is a danger that the past seems a bit too golden. There are a few too many smiles and not enough of the darker side of life. We don't see pictures documenting the worry and anxiety of making ends meet. Winter in the Finger Lakes is long, cold and too drab. Our weather was immortalized by the old-time folk-rock group, the Horseflies. In their song, "I Live Where It's Gray," the songwriter proclaims, "I will never get skin cancer," and then bemoans that "I have legs as white as a priest's." Winter, that seems to last from November through March, is mostly missing from this collection of photographs.

Some of the aspects of life in Tompkins County, such as the soundtrack of the region, are difficult to present in a book of photographs. Behind, beneath and around everything else is music—lots of music. It is a surprise, in a way, that there are not more photographs of the bands, concerts, dancers and informal music that are a part of life here. Is this another accident of history or of historical collections? Jazz, old-time music, rock, folk, classical—all types of music ring through the hills of Tompkins County. Our towns were home to cornet bands, church choirs, square dance bands and glee clubs. Conservatory students from Ithaca College have made their mark ever since the 1890s. The county has had religious revival singers, and it was a center of the folk revival. Live music is still heard at the Ellis Hollow Fair, Dryden Dairy Days, Newfield Old Home Days and at the wonderfully exuberant and popular Grassroots Festival in Trumansburg.

The founding of churches takes an honored place among the signature moments of every community. Early settlers first gathered in private homes to support one another's spiritual well-being and quickly funded and built houses of worship. Today, Tompkins County has a strong and vibrant spiritual life with centers and resources for people of every persuasion—and for those with no denomination. And yet, there are few extant photos of church congregations, Sunday school classes, revival meetings or spiritual activity of any kind. Except for special cases, we don't often photograph our spiritual practices. Considering that, it is thrilling to see the picture of the congregation of the Calvary Baptist Church, located on North Albany Street in the City of Ithaca.

Politics and social activism have always been an important part of Tompkins County's cultural life, and yet few images of these actions are available for the years 1870–1960. Antiwar movements, environmental activism and antitax protests echo the causes of earlier eras—abolitionism, women's suffrage and temperance. It's hard to think of Ithaca and its surrounding communities without thinking of the social causes so dear to the hearts of many. Whether on the left, the right or somewhere in the middle, Tompkins County residents have something to say, and they fully exercise their right to say it. DeWitt Park and the Commons may be our version of London's Hyde Park Speaker's Corner, but there have been political action and activist forums in other towns as well.

Images of ethnic solidarity and celebration are even rarer. The stories of Tompkins County's Finns, Italians, Tibetans, Latinos, Chinese, Koreans and Vietnamese are largely missing from our history. In the case of some, the historical record appears to be thin. For others, such as the Tibetans and Koreans, their period of immigration and population was yet to come—as they arrived in Tompkins County after the 1970s, beyond the historical range of this book.

Even the chroniclers of our history are an accidental group. The Municipal Historians of Tompkins County is a diverse group of men and women, all drawn to working with local history. Town historians, archivists, writers and enthusiastic volunteers—all are keepers of the past. Their diverse interests include railroads, early industry, settlements that have disappeared, new immigrant communities, agriculture and barns, graveyards and the Underground Railroad. Working with this group is always fascinating. It has an infectious enthusiasm for images and stories, gathering the bits of trivia that eventually combine with and contribute to the whole. The days spent sharing and sorting pictures drawn from every corner of the county were punctuated by murmurs of "Ooh, look at this one." The selection of images was dynamic and collaborative, reflecting the combined interests of over two dozen people.

Community and Relationships

My favorite chapter of the book is "In Harmony." In these images we see something specific and, indeed, important. These are moments that capture the social bonds holding us together through time. They are the stuff of lifelong connections, as exemplified by the "Old School Girls" who gathered for a group photo on a summer day in 1951. Twenty-five women "of a certain age," dressed in short-sleeved floral print dresses, squinting into the sun. These women had been friends since they graduated from Dryden High School. The annual summer reunion began gathering graduates from the 1870s and continues now over one hundred years later.

Living here, I know that the more things change, the more they stay the same. This was a rural county in 1870, and for the most part, it still is. I cook with fruits and vegetables grown on local farms just as people have done for decades. Small towns are finding ways to sustain themselves and their surrounding communities by means of a variety of specific activities, tasks and pleasures that sustain us as individuals. We're turning back to a sense of *local*, with neighborhoods and community centers. This is not just a green trend but a way of life with deep roots.

Jane Dieckmann observes in her *Short History of Tompkins County*, that over the course of history there "are qualities that endure: a sense of flexibility and adaptability to the surroundings, the courage to change and the will to persevere, the vision to create something original and significant." An active life is the norm in this corner of the Finger Lakes. County residents fill every night of the week with yoga classes, recitals and music jams, writing groups, book groups or a workout at the gym. Friends zoom from one meeting to the next, juggling four or five or six projects all at once. They complain about how packed their lives are, but they won't consider dropping anything. Each project is a beloved priority in their lives. After all, efforts such as rebuilding houses, ensuring adequate public transportation and adding to the well-being of one's neighbors are all valuable. Taking part in community projects brings joy and satisfaction.

A sense of comfort and ease with the realities of time and place shines through the faces portrayed in this book. These are people who are comfortable with themselves and with one another. These are not, generally, puffed up people. But neither are they downtrodden. They're making the best of what they have. The people in these photos are having a good time, no matter what they're doing.

How do these pictures, these stories, these faces of people long gone add to who we are today? I see them as guiding lights. The expressions on the faces of two older couples playing cards together show me my future. There is a sense of simplicity and stability in the way a man stands with the horses that have been his work companions for twenty years. The photos of these people, all of them working and playing together, are a reminder of who we were…and who we are today.

We could not connect the past to the present without the background information collected and preserved by local historians, the team of guides who know the stories behind the people and places of this book. The short accounts accompanying each photo—identifying people, places, what's really going on—help us understand and have a deeper appreciation of our communities and neighbors, both past and present. The most important things, all of the shared joy and work that create a bigger community, don't change. These are the memories that make us who we are.

–Pamela Goddard

ABOUT THE AUTHORS

Louise Bement was born in northwestern Pennsylvania and has lived in New York State since 1954, when she moved to Bath to teach junior high school at Haverling High School. In 1968, she began her master's degree program at Elmira College, getting her degree in 1972. Moving to the Town of Lansing in 1969, she began her nineteen-year career as a Lansing fourth-grade teacher. She became interested in local history when she and her class researched the Village of Portland Point for their bicentennial project. This class and three others produced local history books that made it logical for Louise to seek the position of town historian in 1981, a position she has held for twenty-eight years. Retiring from teaching in 1989, she founded the Lansing Historical Association. She has continued writing local history in booklets and newsletters and enjoys researching Lansing's history.

Bruce Brittain was born and raised in the scenic and historic hamlet of Forest Home in the Town of Ithaca. He attended the three-room Forest Home School through the third grade, when the school was closed. Bruce earned bachelor's degrees in psychology and mechanical engineering from Bucknell University and a master's and PhD in agricultural engineering from Cornell University. He has taught a variety of technical subjects at both Cornell and Ithaca College. In addition to serving as Forest Home's volunteer historian, he has been involved with many neighborhood preservation activities, including the listing of the Forest Home Historic District on the State and National Registers of Historic Places; the designation of Forest Home Drive as a scenic road in the New York State Scenic Roads Program; the preservation of the hamlet's two single-lane truss bridges; and, most recently, the Forest Home Traffic Calming Project. Bruce has a keen interest in old barns. He still lives in the house in which he grew up.

Pat Brhel was born in Johnson City, New York, in the hospital that a great-grandfather helped found. Pat's first encounter with a historic photo was her grandparents' wedding picture, which she now has hanging on the wall. She had a father who loved fishing and hunting, dragging her to Alaska when she was a teenager to build log cabins and live the life of a pioneer. After 28 years, three children, lots of travel and many adventures, she left Alaska in 1997 and moved to the Town of Caroline, where she bought and began renovating a 160-year-old house and gardens. She has settled down to a relaxing (not really—but it is fun!) retirement as the Caroline deputy historian, Caroline Food Pantry co-director, Brooktondale Community Center chair, Caroline Farmers Market manager and part-time writer and photographer. She enjoys all of these activities but especially likes spending time with her children, daughters-in-law and two grandchildren. Pat shares her home with a rabbit, two parakeets and her newest roommate, a three-month-old puppy.

Alan Chaffee was born in the Town of Newfield and graduated from Newfield Central School in 1964 and then from Alfred State College in 1966. He has worked in management for Wilcox Press, now called Vanguard Printing, with a specialty in paper buying. Alan became interested in Newfield history while in high school; he also received encouragement and information from his grandmother. He was appointed Newfield town historian in 1973 and has nurtured the town's historical society. Alan has compiled a thorough record of all grave markers in 140 cemeteries in Tompkins, Schuyler and Chemung Counties. He has also dismantled a tobacco barn built in the 1880s and rebuilt it in Newfield. He is working on a history of Newfield; his life goals are to please God and to be a good husband and father to his three children.

Jean Currie is currently the interim director of The History Center in Tompkins County. She was a founding member of the Newfield Historical Society and has worked with The History Center in various capacities for many years, most recently as vice-president of the board of trustees. Until she retired in 2008, Jean was the executive director of the South Central Regional Library Council, a multi-type library consortium serving libraries in a fourteen-county area of Upstate New York. She grew up and was educated in New Zealand and has worked in academic, corporate and medical libraries, as well as library consortia, in New Zealand, Australia, Canada and the United States. Jean has lived in the Ithaca area since 1979 and worked at both Cornell and the South Central Regional Library

Council. She has a bachelor of arts degree from Canterbury University in Christchurch, New Zealand, and a Diploma of Library Science from the New Zealand Library School.

Nancy Dean is the deputy historian for the Town of Ulysses and a native of Tompkins County. She attended the two-room school in Jacksonville until eighth grade and then rode the school bus to Trumansburg Central School, which she attended for five years, graduating in 1959. For a sixth-grade school project, Nancy researched historical information on Jacksonville, about which not much had been published. She continued her interest with a senior history honors paper about Jacksonville history. This background led to working for forty-five years at Cornell University Library's Department of Manuscripts and University Archives. Nancy's other interests include photography and the documentation of local events.

Karen Dickson's three great-great-grandfathers were pioneers in the towns of Ulysses and Enfield. Karen grew up in Ulysses on the family farm. She married her high school sweetheart and moved around the state with him until he retired from the New York State Electric and Gas Company. Since then, Karen has concentrated on family genealogy, spurred by thirty years of diaries kept by her great-grandfather Asahel Lovell Harvey in the 1800s. She offeres genealogical aid to people in the community and to women seeking admission to the Daughters of the American Revolution. She became historian for the Town of Ulysses in 2006 and enjoys helping others find their family roots, taking pictures of family homesteads and gravestones in local cemeteries. She is a member of the Ulysses Historical Society and is currently regent of Chief Taughannock Chapter of the DAR.

Terry Donlick has lived in Tompkins County most of her life, growing up in Caroline Depot in the Town of Caroline, where she developed a love for small communities. After living in the Philadelphia area for seven years, Terry and her husband settled in the Town of Groton, where Richard opened a family medicine practice and Terry assisted in the administration of that practice. Terry became deputy historian for the Town of Groton in 2009 and is the owner/innkeeper of Bountiful Blessings Bed & Breakfast on Lick Street, in the Village of Freeville. She is a member of Columbian Club, Groton Town Planning Board, Groton Business Association and the Groton Rotary Club, for which she serves on the District Committee for Youth Exchange as the country contact for Poland. Her love of history has motivated her to remain involved with preserving our county's past.

Donna Eschenbrenner moved to Ithaca with her husband and two sons in 1990. She started working at the History Center in Tompkins County (then the DeWitt Historical Society) as a volunteer to the archivist in 1999. Shortly after that, she was hired as an assistant on the Historic Treasures Unwrapped! project, a successful rehousing initiative for the organization's three-dimensional object collection. But her real love was for the archives, and she became archivist in 2001. She devotes her spare time to her family, running and reading, mostly science books. She is a member of the Tompkins County Water Resources Council.

David George is the assistant historian for the Town of Ithaca. He has supervised local high school students researching the early history of the town and has served on the town's history committee. He grew up in Ithaca and studied archaeology at Cornell University, and he has worked on archaeological projects in New York, Arizona, New Mexico, Italy and Japan. He teaches English to international students and visiting researchers and enjoys hiking, cross-country skiing and traveling with his family.

Pamela Goddard was born in Hanover, New Hampshire, and moved to the Town of Danby in the winter of 1989. The granddaughter of a Dartmouth College history professor, Goddard has always been attracted to local history for the richness of its stories and the way local history can mirror our current lives. After nearly twenty years of educating people of all ages in history museums, Pamela turned to writing about current events for regional newspapers and magazines. She also enjoys sharing timeless stories set to music and has recorded two CDs of traditional songs and ballads. Goddard spends quiet days in her house in the woods, contemplating why people do what they do, in the company of her husband and two cats.

Joan Frost Grant is a resident of the Town of Danby. She was born and raised in Ithaca and has always been fascinated with the city's history and with antiques. Her interest expanded to the Town of Danby, and she was appointed town historian in 2001. Joan enjoys writing a monthly history column for the *Danby Area News* and working with the county historians and the public. She has worked as a registered nurse and as a substitute teacher in health education. She and her husband, Roger, own and operate Grant's Plants Greenhouse in Danby and live with their orange cat Ralphie, dog Bear and parrots Timmy and Bailey.

Roger Warren Grant is a native of Philadelphia, New York, who found his way to Ithaca as an undergraduate at Cornell University. He moved to Danby upon graduation and is currently the town's deputy historian. Roger grew up in a house full of antiques with a family who had a great appreciation for their beauty and utility. He and his wife are the owners of Grant's Plants in Danby and Roger is an assistant chief with the Danby Volunteer Fire Company. He enjoys biking and participates in the AIDS Ride for Life.

Elsie Gutchess spent her childhood in Dryden, often with camera in hand. She lived in Skaneateles and ran an old-fashioned toy and penny candy store, the Toy Peddler. After moving to Cortland, she developed Great Women of the USA, an informational company, and offered programs about interesting and important women across the country. To support herself and children, and a monstrous Victorian house needing restoration, she started Victorian Sales, a household liquidation and antique appraisal business that she ran for twenty-five years. Retiring to Dryden Village, she took on the restoration of a Greek Revival–style house. She served on the board of the Town of Dryden Bicentennial Committee in 1997 and was the historian for the Town of Dryden. She is always gathering local history for future programs and publications and works to make Dryden a vibrant community.

Ellen "Ellie" Hobbie was raised in Sodus, New York, where her parents were charter members of the Sodus Bay Historical Society. She went to Cornell University, majoring in classical civilizations and archaeology, and Durham University in Durham, England, where she was in the Anglo-Saxon and Viking Studies program. She now lives in the Town of Enfield with her two children and assorted animals. She was a charter member of the Enfield Historical Society and is deputy town historian.

Laura Johnson-Kelly is town historian for the Town of Ithaca and also works with archaeological collections at Cornell University as a conservator/photographer. She has a BA from Cornell University and an MA from the University of Michigan–Ann Arbor. Laura has excavated at historic and prehistoric archaeological sites throughout New York State, as well as in Massachusetts, Ohio, Michigan, Nebraska, Colorado, New Mexico, Peru, Chile, Bolivia, Argentina, Greece and Hungary. She lives with her family on the homestead purchased by her great-grandparents in 1908, where she raises blue corn, purple potatoes and chickens that lay green eggs.

Carol Kammen is the appointed Tompkins County historian. She came to Ithaca in 1965. She taught local history at Tompkins Cortland Community College and for twenty-five years at Cornell University. She recently wrote *Ithaca: A Brief History* (2008) and *Peopling of Tompkins County: A Social History*. She has also written *Cornell: Glorious to View*, *First Person Cornell* and *Part and Apart: The African American Experience at Cornell*, in addition to books about local history: *On Doing Local History*, in several editions, and *Pursuit of Local History*. She was named New York Public Historian of 2005–6 and received the American Association for State and Local History Award of Distinction followed by a Tompkins County resolution (#191) in recognition of her work. She lives with her husband and a cat named Tess of the Storm Country. She is working on a book about women and place in Central New York State and revising the *Encyclopedia of Local History*.

Barbara Mix Kone spent the first third of her life in the Town of Caroline, the second third following her military husband around the world and the latest third back in Caroline. She has instilled in her family an appreciation for the first families in the town. She often says that a history of a locality is a history of its people. She has been interested in family history since age fourteen, and that interest has continued to develop over the years. Besides being town historian, she is the president of the Caroline Grove Cemetery, chair of the Caroline Community Library Advisory Committee, postmaster relief at the Slaterville Springs Post Office, the organist at her church, a Sunday school teacher, wife, mother (of seven), grandmother of an increasing number, likes to paint flowers on rocks and thoroughly enjoys life.

Joan Manning is the historian for the Village of Freeville, located in the Town of Dryden. Her office is in the Village Hall, 5 Factory Street. Joan graduated from Dryden High School and attended Alfred State Technical Institute. She has lived in Freeville her entire life and represents the fourth generation of her family to live within three houses of the lower four corners. Joan has been village historian for nineteen years and has presented talks, created walking tours and made slide presentations for the school and local organizations. She specializes in collecting historical documents and photographs of the village and surrounding area. Her hobbies are sketching, gardening and birding. Joan is a member of the Association of Public Historians of New York State, the Dryden Town Historical Society, The History Center in Tompkins County, the Municipal Historians of Tompkins County and the Freeville United Methodist Church.

Michael J. McGandy is a resident of the City of Ithaca. Born in New Brunswick, New Jersey, and a sixteen-year resident of New York City, Michael moved to Ithaca from Brooklyn in December 2007. A position at Cornell University Press brought him to the city. At the press, Michael acquires books in American history, politics and law, with more than an occasional book on New York State history thrown into the mix. His interest in local history is in part professional, as he is always curious to talk to people who are developing book projects of interest to readers in the region and beyond. But local history is also about building and maintaining communities, and that keeps him involved as a volunteer at The History Center in Tompkins County.

Phyllis McNeill was born in Ithaca, New York. She spent her early years in Schuyler County, returning as a child to Ithaca, to which she has been devoted—to its history, its constant development and its daily happenings. She has researched the history of the Town of Ithaca, contributed to the *Place Names of Tompkins County* and has continued to attend regular Municipal Historians of Tompkins County meetings. She graduated from Tompkins Cortland Community College and the University of Binghamton. She has two children, four grandchildren and one great-granddaughter.

Wayne Myers has lived in Danby all his life and in the family house at 1071 Michigan Hollow Road for fifty years. He graduated from the Spencer-Van Etten High School in 1968 and received a bachelor of science degree in animal science from Cornell University in 1972. He has worked for Jim Ray Mobile Homes for more than thirty-six years and has built and maintained large perennial gardens, a water wheel–driven feed mill and a blacksmith shop to display antique tools on his property. With a group of friends who all had ancestors who lived on Bald Hill in Danby, he is engaged in writing a history of Bald Hill that is now a part of the Danby State Forest. In the course of work on this project, the group has located and copied over five hundred photographs of the surrounding area.

Rosemary Rowland was born and raised in Bergen County, New Jersey, before moving to Newfield almost twenty years ago. Before that, she had enlisted in the navy, and she and her husband traveled across the country and overseas. Her daughter, Kelly, was born in Iceland. Rosemary worked as a nurse and devoted time to disability issues, but a passion for genealogy and local history prevailed, and she obtained a certificate in genealogical studies from the National Institute of Genealogical Studies/

University of Toronto. In Newfield, she runs a genealogy study group and manages the town's archives. She has recently become deputy historian. She enjoys beaches and wineries.

Robert C. Snyder graduated from Spencer Central School and State University of New York–Cortland. He is currently doing historical research for Spencer and Danby, in particular researching histories of Spencer's rural district schools. From 1970 to 1975 he lived in Lancaster County, Pennsylvania, and taught in Amish one-room schools. For six years he taught English as a Second Language in Saudi Arabia, and Bob has been a substitute teacher in local schools. He has traveled to many foreign lands and has a special love for some of the remote Pacific Islands. Traveling has given him a respect for indigenous peoples and cultures.

Sue Thompson was born and raised in the Town of Danby. She inherited her interest in genealogy and local history from her mother, documenting and visiting places connected with her family. She enjoys visiting and documenting cemeteries, especially noting unusual gravestones. She has been historian for the Town of Enfield since 1995 and has worked to promote an awareness and appreciation for history. She is employed as an administrative assistant at Cornell University, is the webmaster for the Town of Enfield and chair of the Cemetery Committee in Enfield. She lives with her husband and extended family along with ducks, hamsters, a pixie frog, fish, cats and dogs. Sue enjoys needlework, painting, drawing and cartooning.

Rosemarie Palmer Tucker graduated from Groton Central School in 1966. Appointed historian by January 2001, she is a member of the Association of Public Historians of New York State, Town of Groton Historical Association and the Groton Rotary Club. As a member of the Municipal Historians of Tompkins County, Rosemarie wrote the chapter on Groton for *Place Names of Tompkins County* and wrote "Touring the Towns of Tompkins County: Destination Groton." She has been involved with family and local history research since 1975. Rosemarie has provided articles and pictures for the *Groton Independent* and given talks to the Groton Rotary Club, the elementary school, the Upstate History Alliance and the History Center of Tompkins County. She is currently working on a book titled *Images of America: Groton*. Rosemarie has three brothers, one son, one daughter, two granddaughters and five grandsons. She lives in the house her father built in 1950.

New York state law requires that all villages, towns, cities, counties and the five boroughs of New York City appoint an official historian. The nine towns and six villages in Tompkins County have appointed historians. The position for the City of Ithaca is currently vacant. Although some historians are missing from the picture, many of the people who assisted with this book are included here. *Seated, from left*: Nancy Dean, Rosemary Rowland, Joan Grant, Elsie Gutchess and Louise Bement. *Middle row, from left*: Michael McGandy, Barbara Kone, Joan Manning, Carol Kammen and Donna Eschenbrenner. *Back row, from left*: David George, Alan Chaffee, Pamela Goddard, Laura Johnson-Kelly, Rosemarie Tucker, Bruce Brittain, Ellie Hobbie and Sue Thompson. *Photo taken by Michael Eschenbrenner, June 13, 2009.*

The History Center in Tompkins County was formed in 1935 as a revival of two earlier historical societies of 1863–64 and 1899–1905. The first, the Ithaca Historical and Scientific Society, was started by Ezra Cornell and lasted for less than two years. The DeWitt Historical Society was first formed in 1899 to promote Tompkins County history and was named in honor of Simeon DeWitt, a prominent early Ithacan. The society met to hear papers, erect commemorative plaques and start a collection of books and objects that were housed at the public library after the society disbanded in 1905.

In 1935, members of prominent families revived the organization "to encourage research into local history and preserve objects and documents of historical significance." It collected locally relevant objects, books and documents, mounted exhibits and published articles in the *Ithaca Journal*. It was housed in a room in a local bank before moving to the county courthouse in 1936 and since then has received some support from the county. From 1943 to 1973 the society, located in the Old Courthouse in downtown Ithaca, was open to the public on a regular basis and sometimes had paid staff. Almost the entire collection was on display and could be handled by visitors. The society collected heavily over those years, both items relating to Tompkins County and more generalized artifacts. It published short books on local history and quarterly newsletter, all on its own press.

In 1973, the society moved to the Clinton House, tripled its space and hired its first professionally trained director. It grew steadily, mounted regular exhibits, offered a wide variety of programming and refined its collection policy to more accurately reflect its original focus on Tompkins County.

In 1992–93, the society moved yet again to the former Dean of Ithaca Building (later the Gateway Plaza) and into renovated museum space. In 2004, the DeWitt Historical Society was renamed The History Center in Tompkins County. This name change and a new strategic plan resulted in more focused attention on the educational and research activities of the organization.

The History Center offers regular exhibits, formal and informal talks, a strong program of educational activities for children and adults, publication of books and regular articles in the *Ithaca Journal*, reference services from the library and archives and an increasing presence on the Web. The History Center is a member of the Discovery Trail and Kids Discover the Trail, and through our unique program at the Eight Square School House, fourth graders can attend school in 1892. In addition, it has robust connections to the high schools and the colleges in the county with programs that link local history to classes in history and the environment. It also offers a space to host public discussion on contemporary issues, a place for civic engagement at which issues and questions can be viewed through the lens of history.

Special thanks goes to the volunteers at The History Center who were so helpful: Alison Maceli, Louise Matosich, Mari Tiwari, Janet Wagner, Jane Marcham, Brittany Bovenzi, Desiree Alexander and Dylan Schoch.